LIVING A SECOND LIFE
A SOBER LIFE

JOSEPH HARRINGTON

LIVING A SECOND LIFE, A SOBER LIFE

DEDICATION

This book is dedicated to the still-sick and suffering alcoholic and to all the groups that help the still-sick and suffering find the help they need. A special thank you and dedication to my homegroup, The Drunk Squad, for their commitment to service and healthy living.

MEMORIAL DEDICATION

This dedication is being added to my book. As I was in the final editing stages and getting ready for publishing of this book, my family suffered a loss. The matriarch of our family Mary Miller passed away. She was my mother in law. She was a great mother of 3 children, grandmother of 7 grandchildren, great grandmother of 6 great grandchildren and a friend to all she met. She never really had a lot but she would tell you she always had everything she needed. She showed everyone how to love unconditionally, she always accepted everyone for who they were and loved them. Even in my darkest of days she loved me and accepted me when I was incapable of loving myself. Mary was like a mom to me, she will never know how much she taught me. Her family was her world and she passed that down to all of us. She embodied the saying "live everyday as though it was your last". She never wanted much, she just wanted to see her family be happy and love each other. She will be greatly missed and she will always be loved. I am grateful that I was able to add this to my book before it was published. I love you Mary, God Bless.

Table of Contents

INTRODUCTION

This is my experience, my story. As a suffering alcoholic, I thought there was no way out, but that turned out to be just one of the many misconceptions I had. I hope you find something in the words of this book that will spark the life inside you to have the courage to explore the wonderful life sobriety can offer you. I found sobriety through the program offered by Alcoholics Anonymous. I do not speak on AA's behalf or represent AA. My story includes AA and my journey to a better and sober life through that program of recovery. I hope you will find something in my words that will help you with whatever problem you are having. Many people have had to find their way through the darkness of addiction to find the light of life. My story is just one of the millions of similar stories. The main goal in reading a story like this is to try and identify with the feelings I struggled with rather than compare the outside results of my drinking days.

The words on our pages may be different, but our stories are the same. The AA program has gotten millions sober and greatly improved their lives since the very early days of the original Drunk Squad.

The Drunk Squad is the group name given to the first group of Alcoholics Anonymous that dates back to the very early days of Alcoholics Anonymous. This group would meet starting in the fall of 1935 in the home of Bill and Lois Wilson at 182 Clinton St in Brooklyn, New York. Bill Wilson is one of the founders of AA; in those days, there were only about 40 members of AA; today, there are over two million.

There wasn't a large fellowship of recovering alcoholics the way there is today, there wasn't even a Big Book of Alcoholics Anonymous. There was just an opinion offered by a Doctor who worked with alot of drunks as to why an alcoholic is alcoholic and different from heavy and social drinkers when it came to their drinking. Which is the first time anyone had an opinion of alcohol being a disease and an opinion as to what the disease consisted of. And there were the 4 absolutes of the Oxford Group which were Absolute Honesty, Absolute Purity, Absolute Unselfishness and Absolute Love. Which would become the foundation for the steps as we know them today and the yardsticks by which to measure our lives.

The group I belong to adopted that same name, The Drunk Squad. I have the gift of sobriety today because of the original Drunk Squad and the work they did in the early days, as well as the work the Drunk Squad I belong to does alongside every other AA group, in carrying the message of hope to the suffering alcoholic.

Perhaps the same can happen for you. This book starts off like a typical AA meeting, then moves to my personal experience with my addiction, and then an explanation of the program that I credit today for having changed my life. There are some stories of others who have also sought a better way of living. All the people and stories in this book are real, and the results are real. May you find your truth in our stories and seek the path we took so you, too, can have the life we have found.

Chapter 01

FROM THE PODIUM

My name is Joe, and I am an alcoholic. It is always great to be in a meeting with Alcoholics Anonymous; it's always an honor to share my experience, strength, and hope with the people I know.

But when I say experience strength and hope, I am not talking about my drunk-a-log; I don't do that; the people who know me know I don't do that, and honestly, it's not that interesting anyway. I am talking about my experience working the steps of Alcoholics Anonymous, the strength I gained as I worked the steps of Alcoholics Anonymous, and the hope I have for today and tomorrow as a result of those steps and as I continue to apply them to everything in my life.

When I say the people I know. I may not know your first name or favorite color, but if you're an alcoholic in a meeting of Alcoholics Anonymous tonight. I know the bumpy road you took to get here, the mental pain, the emotional struggles you had to endure to even make alcoholics anonymous as an option to help you. I know the fear and uncertainty that accompanies you when you come across that threshold the very first time. I also know the desperation and hope for a better life that gives you the courage to make it across that threshold.

The words on our pages may be different, but our story is the same, so yes, I know you, and you know me.

My sobriety date is June 25th, 2015, or as I call it, the day I started to be restored to sanity. When I came across that threshold the first time, full of fear and uncertainty, the idea the notion that I needed to be restored to sanity was not on my list of things to do. I just wanted to stop drinking.

In fact, when I saw your second step up on the wall, I figured that had to be for everyone else because it certainly didn't apply to me.

You see despite that fact, I dropped out of high school my senior year because partying was far more interesting than studying. I owned a very successful company when I entered the halls of Alcoholics Anonymous and had not yet experienced some of the financial struggles some of us do. Despite the fact I chose to drive drunk every day, I had not yet acquired a DUI to my credit when I entered the halls of Alcoholics Anonymous. Despite the fact my alcoholism held me prisoner every day, I had not yet spent any time in a jail cell as a result of my drinking when I came into the halls of Alcoholics Anonymous and despite the fact I always chose my relationship with my alcohol over my relationships with my family and loved ones, I had not yet lost any of those relationships. Do not misunderstand me. I seriously damaged them all, but I had not yet lost any of those relationships when I came into the halls of Alcoholics Anonymous.

So, the thought that I needed to be restored to sanity wasn't there. But then one day, while I was working in the Big Book of Alcoholics Anonymous, I came across a reference to sanity in the Doctor's Opinion. The doctor referenced sanity as the ability to see the truth from the false, which interested me. As an alcoholic, I always had my own version of the truth, but I needed to understand what truth really meant.

I went to a source that contains the meaning of all words, the dictionary. When I looked up the definition of truth, two words jumped off the page at me as synonymous with truth. One of those words was a fact. If it's true, then it's a fact; if it's a fact, then it's the truth. Well, that made sense. But when it came to my drinking, I didn't make my decisions based on facts. I made my decisions based on my feelings. How I felt about all the people in my life, how I felt about all the situations going on in my life, and probably more importantly, how I felt about myself inside.

The other word synonymous with truth was reality or real. If it's real, then it's true; if it's the truth, then it's reality. That also made sense. But when it came to my drinking, I didn't make my decisions based on reality. I made my decisions based on fantasies. I imagined how all the people in my life could be, how all the situations in my life would be if everyone would only listen to me.

So when I saw that definition and honestly applied it to my life, I could only come to one conclusion. That when it came to my thinking about my drinking, I would indeed need to be restored to sanity, and I would start that journey on June 25th, 2015.

But on June 24th, I would stand at the doorstep of sanity. I would even peek through the window of sanity. But I wouldn't go in. Now, June 24th wasn't different from any other day up until that time. I woke up like I did every morning, hungover. I quickly got my friend's guilt, shame, and remorse up, as I would need them if I was going to get through the day, and I made my way to the shower to get ready for work. While I was in that shower, I repeated another daily ritual. I promised myself that today I wasn't going to drink. Haven broke that promise the day before that, the weeks before that, the months before that, and even the years before that.

I had been making that promise to myself in that shower every day for a very long time. Unable to keep that promise, always breaking that promise. I don't know about any of you, but I do not like when people break promises to me. I get upset, I get angry, I get resentments. And because I was the only one doing any promise-breaking in this scenario, I had been working on the most dangerous resentment of all resentments: self-resentment. The dangerous thing about self-resentment is it cannot exist on the same plane as self-esteem. So, the more I worked on my self-resentment, the less self-esteem I had. Standing in that shower that morning, I didn't like myself, I didn't trust myself, and I certainly didn't believe in myself. But because I live in a world of fantasies and feelings, I would make that promise yet again; today would be different; today, the moon, the stars, and the planets would fall into some perfect alignment, and today, I wouldn't drink. My friends, that's just pure insanity.

I would finish up in the shower, and as I was getting ready for work, I would catch my eyes in the mirror. I hadn't looked into my eyes in some time. But I saw darkness and emptiness, a look I can only describe as hopelessness. I didn't recognize the person looking back at me. I knew as soon as I saw that it was a direct result of my drinking.

I knew I had to do something about my drinking. It would only take me a couple minutes to come up with a plan of exactly what I needed to do. You see, after everyone had gone to bed in my house at night, I was allowed to drink the way I wanted to drink towards my next blackout. From time to time, I would grab my laptop and look up how to stop drinking; yes, you heard that right, I would look up how to stop drinking while drinking because, hey that's sane. But I had read about Antabuse and how Antabuse had helped others stop drinking. So that was the answer. I just needed to get myself some Antabuse, and I knew exactly how I could do that. A very good friend of mine was my doctor; surely he would write me a prescription for Antabuse.

So that's what I would do. I stopped by my doctor's office on my way to work that morning without an appointment because everyone does that. When my doctor friend was able to see me, I told him of some of the problems I was having with my drinking and that I needed him to write me a prescription for Antabuse. I didn't tell him everything; he only needed to know enough to write a prescription. We talked for about thirty minutes or so. During that conversation, he told me about a friend of his who recently celebrated 25 years of sobriety in the halls of Alcoholics Anonymous. As he told me the story, all I could think was, that's nice. I don't know what that has to do with what we are talking about, but good for him. When we were done talking, my friend reached down to his desk for what I thought was his prescription pad. But when his hand came up, he had a business card in it. The business card was for AdCare. He handed me the card and said, "Joe, I want you to call the number on this business card; these people specialize in behavioral issues." I got instantly annoyed. Clearly, my friend hadn't been listening to me. I don't have a behavior problem; I have a drinking problem. But I took the card, and on the way out of his office, I stuffed it in my pocket with absolutely no intention of calling the number on that card.

I got in my car and started to make my way to my office. I would get about two blocks from my doctor's office, and suddenly, the thought came into my head that maybe, maybe, I should just call the number on that business card. So I pulled into a parking lot and dialed the number on the card. When the lady answered, I explained to her that my doctor had recommended I call her as I had gone to see him because I was having problems with my drinking. She asked me some questions about my drinking. I answered them a bit more honestly than I had been with my doctor.

After a few minutes, she asked me if I'd be willing to call a colleague of hers in South Kingstown; well, I was waist-deep in it by now, so I agreed to call her. As I dialed the next number, I couldn't help but wonder just how hard it is to get a prescription for Antabuse anyway. When the next lady got on the phone, I told her that her colleague had referred me to her, that I had been referred to her colleague by my doctor, whom I had gone to see about a drinking problem.

She asked me some questions about my drinking, and I answered them as honestly as I could. She became interested in my answers and asked even more questions, and I answered those. She was really interested in what I was saying and wanted to hear more about my drinking, so she invited me to come stay a few days with her. As flattered as I was at the offer, I explained I wouldn't be able to. You see, my daughter and I had signed up for sign language classes, and one of those classes was that night, and I wasn't willing to break that commitment. She respected that and understood, but she still wanted to hear more about my drinking, so she asked me if I would be able to come in the following day, and I agreed.

On my way into my office, I would summon up my friend's Guilt, Shame, and Remorse. I would need them to attend the pity party I was about to host as I told my wife what I was planning to do. I would have that conversation with my wife, crocodile tears and all. I would finish my work day and attend that sign language class with my daughter. When the class ended, my daughter and I would say our goodbyes and head home.

But I would do what any self-respecting alcoholic who was checking themselves into detox the next day would do. I would stop and buy myself some alcohol. Where was that feeling of hopelessness I had that morning? Where was the desperation that had me take the actions I had taken earlier in the day to address my drinking? They weren't there. It was as if it never happened. If that is not an example of insanity, I don't know what is. But I would be a responsible alcoholic when I got home. I would be sure to finish every drop in those bottles; nothing would go to waste.

I would get up the next morning and make my way to AdCare. Once I got checked in and settled in, I made my way to the community room where the other residents were.

I sat down, not knowing anyone. As I was working on a puzzle I started listening to the conversations being had in the room. I started hearing my story in their words. The words on the pages were different, but the story was the same. While I was in AdCare, kind, caring people from Alcoholics Anonymous would come in every night on commitments. They would explain how they were once like us, but because of the program of Alcoholics Anonymous, their lives had gotten better. That interested me. I don't remember any one particular story told. What I do remember is the consistent message every one of those groups left us with. "When you get out of here, go to meetings, join a homegroup, get a job in that homegroup, get a sponsor, and work the program in The Big Book of Alcoholics Anonymous."

I would take them up on those suggestions one at a time. When I got out, I went to a meeting of one of those commitment groups that came in. When I walked across that threshold the first time, full of fear and uncertainty, I saw a man standing at the front of the room who looked important to me. I mean, he was standing at a podium, shuffling some papers so he looked important. I made my way to him and introduced myself to him. He introduced himself as Bill. I asked Bill how does someone go about signing up for one of these groups? Bill picked up a clipboard lying on the podium. He flipped through some pages that seemed to have some names and numbers on them. He stopped at a page then looked my square in the eye and said "we have one opening left in this group, if you'd like it can be yours'. Well momma didn't raise no fool, so I scooped that spot right up. I wrote my first name, sobriety date and phone number down. Bill welcomed me to the group, I thanked Bill for his help and I sat down to my first meeting of Alcoholics Anonymous on June 29th, 2015. As my new found friend Bill opened the meeting he would make some announcements. One of those announcements was "Attention all group members" I was a group member now, Bill was talking to me, "tonight we have a business meeting so please stay after the meeting and tonight we have elections". I felt obligated to stay, I mean I just took the last spot in the group so I needed to stay. But I couldn't help but wonder, what kinda business does a bunch of alcoholics meet about and exactly what seats are they electing people into. I stayed for that meeting and when the job of coffee maker came up, despite never having made a pot of coffee in my life I raised my hand and became the coffee maker, the best job in AA if you ask me.

That night, I had crossed three of the suggestions made to me while I was at AdCare off the list. I only needed to find a sponsor so I could work the program of recovery in The Big Book. I asked one of the men who came in on the commitment at AdCare if he would be my sponsor, and he said yes. I asked him if he would bring me through the program of recovery in the Big Book, and he said yes. But of course, he would. It would be another example of insanity to join a 12-step group and not do the 12 steps.

I love the steps of Alcoholics Anonymous. They changed my life. They saved my life. Don't get me wrong, I love the fellowship of Alcoholics Anonymous. I have made a lot of great friendships in these halls, and I have a lot of real friends in the fellowship. But it is the steps that saved my life. I always like to share my experience with the steps of Alcoholics Anonymous when I share. I think sometimes we make too difficult a task out of such a simple program.

Step 1: Admitted – I was powerless over alcohol, and my life had become unmanageable. This step would take me the longest to complete, literally decades. You see, I didn't become powerless over alcohol in the halls of Alcoholics Anonymous. My life certainly didn't become unmanageable in the halls of Alcoholics Anonymous. That happened while I was out there, doing the things I was doing all those years. I would concede to the powerlessness that morning I gazed in the mirror, seeing that hopelessness. To have no hope is to have no power. I would come to understand why I was powerless in the halls of Alcoholics Anonymous. I would learn of the body allergy of the obsession of the mind in the halls. I would learn that the unmanageability wasn't the lost jobs, the divorce courts, time in jail, or even the DUIs. Those things happen to non-alcoholics, too. The unmanageability from within, the guilt, the shame, the feelings of being less than. And when I did, I was done with Step 1.

Step 2: Came to believe a power greater than myself could restore me to sanity. Well, I didn't have to come to believe in a power greater than myself. I just admitted there was a power greater than myself in Step 1. If I am powerless over alcohol, then alcohol is a power greater than me. I already gave some examples in this story as to how alcohol took away my sanity. I am a believer that for every negative, there is a positive; for every con, there is a pro. So if there is a power greater than I and it took away my sanity, there had to be a power greater than myself that could restore that sanity. Could I believe it? Absolutely, and I was done with Step 2.

Step 3: Made a decision to turn my will and my life over to the care of God as I understood him. Now, I had some problems with this step, mainly with the words used. First of all, do you want me to make a decision? I am an alcoholic. I don't like to make decisions; I get forced into decisions. And you want me to turn my will and my life over? That sounds like an awfully big commitment. I don't think I made that big of a commitment when I got married, well, at least not intentionally. But it would be explained to me that Will simply means to think. To Will something is to think about it. Life is just a collection of my actions over a period of time. So when I looked at that step that way, to turn my thinking and my actions over to the care of God, I could do that. Besides, I saw a shortcut; I know I cannot take any action without first having the thought to do so. I can't pick up a bottle of water without my brain telling my hand to do so. So, if I could do 50% of this step and turn my thinking over to the care of God, my actions should follow, and I was done with Step 3.

Step 4: Made a searching and fearless moral inventory of myself. I had heard a lot about Step 4 since coming into the halls of Alcoholics Anonymous. When to take Step 4, why to take Step 4, and How to take Step 4. I don't understand all the confusion around Step 4. The Big Book, Alcoholics Anonymous' basic text, answers all those questions. As to how to do Step 4, starting on the bottom of page 64, there are step-by-step instructions as to how exactly Step 4 should be taken, line-line instructions. Right before those instructions, we are told exactly why we need to take this step. It says, "When the spiritual malady is overcome, we straighten out mentally and physically." Once we overcome our spiritual sickness, we straighten out mentally, so the obsession of the mind won't become an issue, which means I won't always be thinking about drinking. If I am not always thinking, I am not going to put a drink in my mouth.

If I don't put a drink in my mouth, I won't trigger the body allergy and will have straightened out physically. And as far as when to do Step 4, that is also answered on page 64 at the top. It tells us, "Though our decision (Step 3, page 63) was a vital step, it could have little permanent effect unless at once followed by a strenuous effort". It says at once that's not six months, not three months, not even a month. It means as soon as you have taken Step 3, you begin Step 4.

I don't understand all the confusion around Step 4. Besides, Step 4 is the step I was most prepared for when I came into the halls. If you had asked me when I first came in who I was upset at and who had caused me harm, I could have told you that. If you had asked me what they did to me, I could have told you that. If you had asked me if it affected my self-esteem, my wallet, my relationships, or my ambitions, I could have told you that. If you asked me if I was honest in that situation, if I was being selfish or inconsiderate, I could have told you. If you asked me if I had any fears connected to those situations, I could have told you. I could have told you what I was afraid of losing, what I was afraid I wouldn't get, and what I was afraid you would find out about me. I could have told you all the people I had harmed. I could have told you exactly what I did to them and exactly why I did it. I could have told you all of this the day I came into these halls; it was already in my head. I just needed to learn how to get it out of my head and put it on paper, and once you taught me how to do that, I was done with Step 4.

Step 5: Admitted to God, myself, and another human being the exact nature of my wrongs. Well, God knows everything, so I was concerned there, and I wrote the list to begin with so clearly I know my wrongs. But to have to tell another person about some of this? What is he going to think about me? Well, the answer to that question was nothing. He wouldn't think anything about me based on what we discussed. He would help me understand some of those feelings. You see, the words on his pages were different, but his story was the same. I feared the fifth step more than any other step. But when I was done with that step, I had never felt more free in my life. It was as if the weight of the world had been lifted from my shoulders. And I was done with Step 5.

Step 6: We're entirely ready to have God remove all these defects of character. I would go back to my fourth step and see where I had been dishonest, inconsiderate, and selfish. Where I had made decisions based on fear. I would ask myself, do I like this about me? The simple answer was no. Then I would ask myself if I would like to have God help me to get rid of these things, and the answer was yes, and I was done with Step 6.

Step 7: Humbly asked him to remove my shortcomings. I would do this through prayer. I still do this today. I would ask to be more honest today than I was yesterday. I would ask to have more courage today than I did yesterday, to be more considerate today, a little less selfish today. And I was done with Step 7.

Step 8: Made a list of all the persons we had harmed and became willing to make amends to them all. We already have the list. We made it in our fourth-step inventory. It tells us on page 76, "We have a list of all persons we have harmed and to whom we are willing to make amends. We made it when we took inventory." I guess if you're feeling ambitious, you can make another list, but we already have it.

As long as I was honest and thorough in my inventory, I should have everyone I had harmed listed. But the key here is being willing to make amends. For me, it was easy. I mean, if anyone had done to me some of the things I had done, I would expect them to make amends, so yes, I was willing. And just because I was willing didn't mean I had to run out tomorrow and get it done; I just had to be willing to do it. When I was willing, I was done with step 8.

Step 9: Made direct amends to such people wherever possible, except when doing so would injure them or others. I would break my list into 3 sections: the easy ones, not so easy ones, and the ones I'm never going to. But if I could cause you harm eyeball to eyeball, I should be able to ask for forgiveness eyeball to eyeball. Unless by me doing so, I would cause you or someone else harm by doing so. But even in those scenarios, I would still owe the amends, so if I could do it in a direct fashion, I would need to find another way to make it right indirectly. And sometimes, people move away, and sometimes, they die before we have had a chance to make amends. But again, I still owed it. For me, I found writing a letter to be a good way to handle those situations, but that was me. That was my way. It may be different for you. But when I did this, I was done with Step 9.

Having completed the first nine steps of Alcoholics Anonymous, I have cleaned up a lot of my past. You see, I had been traveling down the highway of life with no destination but always in a hurry to get there. From time to time, I would get hungry, so I would pull off at a truck stop so I could go through the drive-thru to get something to eat and drink. Then, I would jump right back on the road and eat as I drove. When I finished my meal, I would toss my trash into the backseat.

After decades of doing this, every now and then, some idiot driving in front of me would slam on his brakes, forcing me to jam on my brakes. When I did, all that trash from the backseat would come flooding forward into the front seat. The only way I knew how to deal with that was to drink at it. The first nine steps of recovery are like a friend coming over and helping you clean out your car. When I was done with those steps, my car was clean. Now, I needed to learn how to keep it clean, and the next steps would solve that problem.

Step 10: Continued to take personal inventory and, when we were wrong, promptly admitted it. This step is just a neatly packaged steps 4,5,6,7,8, and 9, all wrapped up into one little step. If I continue to take a personal inventory, there will be no build-up of trash or hard feelings. So, as I travel down the highway of life and that idiot jacks up in front of me, all I have to worry about is the car in front of me. I don't need to be concerned about anything from my past, in my backseat, to coming flooding into my day. I will never be done with Step 10. It is one of those things I keep in my daily routine. It keeps me sane; it helps keep me sober.

Step 11: Sought through prayer and meditation to improve (not maintain) our conscious contact with God as we understood Him, praying only for knowledge of His will for us and the power to carry that out. In Step 2, when I came to believe that there was a power greater than myself, I improved my conscious contact with God. In Step 3, when I made a decision to turn my will and my life over to the care of God, I sought His will instead of my own. Step 11 is just an evolving Steps 2 and 3.

Step 12: Having had a spiritual awakening as the result of these Steps, we tried to carry this message to alcoholics and to practice these principles in all our affairs. My life has been saved. I am not the same person today that I was before these steps. I need to do for other alcoholics what those people from AA did for me when I was in AdCare. I need to let other alcoholics know their lives can be better. It is easy to practice these principles when I am in the halls of Alcoholics Anonymous, but it's outside the halls that counts.

Before these steps, I lived in a world of insanity. A definition of insanity is doing the same things over and over again and expecting different results, like making the same promise in the shower day after day. Today, I live in a world of sanity, which for me means doing the same things over and over again and expecting the same results.

I know why my life is how it is today. I know the things I've done to give me a life I never thought possible. I know it is not a result of my thinking, my will. It is a result of these steps and the program of recovery. So today, I will do to the best of my willingness the same things I did yesterday, the day before that, the months before that, and the years before that.

Because of these steps, two years ago, I was able to walk my oldest daughter down the aisle at her wedding sober. I was able to be all emotional in the moment and not care what anyone thought, just enjoy the moment. I was able to have our father-daughter dance at her wedding and today I am able to remember the joy I felt because I was sober. A few months ago, that same daughter gave birth to my wife and my first grandson. And by the grace of my God and as long as I continue to apply these steps on a daily basis, that grandson will never have to see his grandfather drunk, an experience his mother didn't get.

I will always be grateful for the program of recovery and the steps in that program. I will always be grateful to the fellowship of Alcoholics Anonymous for being there when I needed them most. I will always be grateful to my sponsor, Dean, for taking me through the steps that changed my life. I will always be grateful to my friend Bill for giving me that last seat in the group. I will always be grateful to those kind people from Alcoholics Anonymous for coming in on that commitment and letting me know my life could be better when I was in AdCare. I will always be grateful to the other residents of AdCare for allowing me to understand that even though the words on the pages may be different, the story is the same. I will always be grateful to that kind lady who invited me to come spend a few days with her. But most of all, I will always be grateful to my God for putting that thought in my head that maybe, maybe, I should just call the number on that business card.

That is what we in AA call our podium message, the message that lets others know of our journey through sobriety. This has been the way one alcoholic can help another alcoholic, and this way of identification dates back to 1935 when Bill Wilson told his story to Dr. Bob, the founders of AA. It is a high-level satellite view, but as they say, the devil is in the details.

Chapter 02

MY STORY

I didn't become an alcoholic overnight. It takes years of practice to become an alcoholic. Alcoholics, in my opinion, are some of the smartest people around. Think about it. We couldn't get away with the things we do if we weren't smart. I mean the planning, the manipulation just to protect our right to get drunk. If you are reading this book, it's not because you're bored. It may be you are exploring whether you are an alcoholic or not. It may be because you've decided you have a drinking problem and want to understand it. It may also be because a loved one of yours is having a drinking problem, and you're trying to figure out how to help.

In any case, I hope you find what you're looking for. But that means I need to go into deeper details about my own drinking experience as well as the answers I found.

Alcoholism is a serious disease; it is a killer. It attacks the body in ways many of us were not aware of until we sought help through sobriety. The thought of being sober was scary for me. I couldn't imagine what my life would look like without my alcohol to help me through the day. After all, I had included alcohol in my life in the same fashion I had oxygen in my life; without it, I would not suffocate. I never saw myself as an alcoholic. For me, that was the homeless guy in a trench coat grasping onto a brown paper bag. But the truth is alcoholism does not discriminate. Alcoholism doesn't care about your skin color, your age, your education, or how much money you have in the bank. Most will become alcoholics slowly over years and years of drinking. Some will have a faster track to the disease, only having been drinking for a short period of time. But nearly all will never know they are on a deadly path. Most believe they can control their drinking with a little bit of willpower. But if you are truly an alcoholic, you will find that to be an impossible task. It will start to wear on you; you will feel there is something morally wrong with you. You may slip into depression, not understanding why. It will be scary as you start to realize alcohol is winning the fight. This leads to even more drinking, heavier drinking, and hiding your drinking. The idea that you need to learn to live without alcohol will be a scary thought. Sometimes, that fear will hold you back. For most, this will be true. Exploring a new frontier and going out into the unknown is a scary proposition.

Most of our families and friends will not see this as a difficult task; in fact, they hardly understand why we have the problem to begin with. They are not wrong for their feelings or thoughts; they truly just do not understand what it is like to be an alcoholic. Only an alcoholic truly understands those feelings. That is why I have decided to write this book, why I have decided to put my story out for all to see. My story isn't much different from yours. Sure, there may be some differences in the details of living my life. But the emotions and the way I viewed life, in general, will probably resemble your feelings and your views as they relate to your own problems.

I am grateful to be sober today as I write this, but it is not lost on me that there are still a lot of people out there who are sick and suffering from addiction. Literally thousands in every community, tens of thousands in every city, hundreds of thousands in every state, tens of millions across this country, and hundreds of millions worldwide.

Some will never know the opportunity I have been blessed with, the opportunity to live a sober life.

Some will die today not having enjoyed a sober breath for a very, very long time. I heard when I first started my road to sobriety that we have but two options as alcoholics. One is to do the work and get sober; the other is to die of an alcoholic death. At first, that seemed extreme to me, but I can tell you I have witnessed that in reality. One alcoholic dies every four minutes from their disease in the U.S. alone. I have seen people come in and do the work and get better; their family lives improve dramatically, and their lives in general greatly improve. I have also been witness to those who came in, thought it wasn't for them, went back out, and then heard of their deaths. This actually happened to a friend of mine, Tim.

Tim had been battling his disease for many years. I met him when he came to work for me before I got sober. Tim was a great employee, worked hard, and was very productive. One day, he didn't show up to work, which was not normal. Tim didn't call in, so I had no idea what had happened. He would be missing from work for about a week before he showed up again. He explained to me that he had a drinking problem and that he would be doing fine when he went to AA meetings, but then he would stop going and be off again drinking himself into oblivion. Tim had stopped going to his meetings and had relapsed; it took him the entire week he was out drinking to come out of his drunk. As Tim explained his escapades there was a sense of shame and disappointment in the way he discussed it. Eventually, Tim left my company and wouldn't come back for a few years.

By the time Tim made it back to me he was looking to come back and work for me. I had been sober for over 60 days, and had a different thought process when we spoke. I would tell Tim I was an alcoholic and that I was in sobriety, going to meetings and working the steps. Tim would eventually come back and work for me and would actually go to a couple of meetings with me. But he wasn't interested in the steps; he actually was afraid of the steps. Tim would get some time under his belt, being dry for eight months and not working the program. I would celebrate my first year anniversary of being sober, and right before that, Tim would disappear again a week prior to my anniversary. I would get a call on my way to my weekly AA meeting the week after my first year. It was from a number I did not recognize, but I answered it anyway. It was Tim's sister; she said she was calling me because Tim always spoke about me as being helpful to him. She told me Tim had died, he was found in his car in the city, he had drunk and passed out and died from alcohol poisoning.

I was devastated; I couldn't imagine the feeling of loneliness, having relapsed, and the feelings of guilt, shame, and remorse that would lead to him drinking to escape those feelings. To the level he would overdose on booze and die in his backseat. Tim would die never truly understanding the seriousness of his disease; he would die without ever really diving into the life of sober living with the same intensity he dove into his drinking. Many will follow the same path as Tim and eventually end up with the same results as Tim.

Everyone underplays just how dangerous alcohol really is. When I was in detox, I would become aware of the severity of my drinking while detoxing from drinking. If you've never been in a detox facility, let's describe your first day. Your vitals are tracked every couple of hours, including overnight. Yes, I had to be woken up every 2 hours so they could check my vitals. I had to do this while the person I shared my room with who was detoxing from cocaine slept, while the guys in the next room detoxing from heroin slept.

I questioned this and was told that, by far, detoxing from alcohol was the most dangerous substance to detox from. In fact, the more times you go through the process, the more likely a heart attack will occur. Despite the fact I had to wake up while others slept, I wasn't totally convinced this was reality, but rather a scare tactic. But the very next day, a new alcoholic would join us in detox after being released from a local hospital where he had flat-lined while detoxing. It is real. We have but two options: to recover from our alcoholism or die from it. I am blessed to be one of the few who have been given this opportunity, this choice to be sober. I am also blessed to be among the few of the few who stuck around long enough to understand that my worst day sober has been so much better than my best days drunk. I am humbled by the fact someone will die of this disease as I write this, as you read this. I am saddened by the fact that it didn't have to be that way.

Alcoholism has always been here. There are several verses in the proverbs in the bible, which were written before Christ, that describe alcohol and alcoholism, so it was a problem over three thousand years ago, and the problem will always be here. Proverb 23:21 says, "Drunkenness causes poverty." Now that's certainly true today, isn't it? Even 3,000 years later, Proverb 23:29-30 says, "Drinking causes woe, sorrow, fighting, babbling, wounds without cause and red eyes." That also is true today. Even thousands of years later, the description of an alcoholic is the same. Benjamin Rush was one of the signers of the Declaration of Independence. He wrote a paper on alcoholism in 1784; he thought it was a disease but couldn't prove it. Dr. Silkworth came up with his theory on body allergy in 1937. But it wasn't until 1956 that the American Medical Association classified alcoholism as a disease. Thus dispelling the concept that alcoholics were mentally defective or morally deficient.

Today, we live in a time where we not only understand the problem, but today we have a solution. Most who are told of the solution will find excuses as to why that solution is not the right solution for them. Maybe it isn't, but it is a better solution than the one they are using now, so why not use it until they find their "Perfect" solution. I hear many object to the "God" aspect of the recovery program; again, this is an excuse. If you are to be honest with yourself, you must realize your alcohol or your drug of choice is your current God. In recovery, God is simply referred to as "A Power Greater Than Myself." Well, I have no power over my booze; thus, my booze is a power greater than I, and therefore my God.

As I said, this is not an overnight process when it comes to developing the disease side or the sobriety side. The first time I ever took a drink of alcohol was not to get drunk. In fact, my father used it in a medicinal manner. I was about nine years old, and I had a bad toothache for several days. My dad asked me how it felt one night, and I told him it hurt really bad. He had me grab a bottle from under the counter. I don't remember what it was, but I believe it was Seagrams Seven, as that is what I remember my dad drinking back then. He poured some into a glass and told me to hold my nose and drink it; he also told me to swish it around in my mouth. I did as I was told. I don't remember what it tasted like, and I certainly don't recall any great feeling when I drank it. But my toothache didn't hurt as much afterward. I believe right then, at that moment, my brain registered that Alcohol was a solution to that problem.

I didn't wake up the next day tracking down another drink; in fact, I wouldn't drink again until my early teens. It is a typical time when teenagers experiment with things like alcohol, drugs, and sex. But my experiment would look more like scientific research. It would take me over 35 years to complete my experiment. During that time, I would be creating a world that would only feed the fire I had started. This was not a conscious decision but rather one that seemed to evolve naturally. It wouldn't be until I got sober and had some time under my belt that I would be able to see the path behind me more clearly.

My family life was a bit of a shit show as well; my dad was a heavy drinker, which led to a lot of fighting between my parents. Police were often needed to calm the storm in order that my sisters and I could actually get some sleep. This was embarrassing and created more of those feelings of being different than the people I hung out with. I mean, how many stories can you possibly come up with to your friends to explain why the police are always at your house? The reality was that I was the one who would crawl out my bedroom window and sneak to the neighbor's house to call the police. Being woken up night after night to screaming and crashing furniture would instill fear into anyone. The ironic part is there were good times, happy times in that same household. The only times things were really bad was when Dad drank; now, you would think this would be a strong warning to an up-and-coming alcoholic, but unfortunately, it was not.

Everyone in the neighborhood knew that our house was troubled, and some of my friends would not be allowed to hang out with me. In a small neighborhood, that was equivalent to solitary confinement. Other friends were left to balance who would be included in things like pool parties in the summer or just hanging out. My social circle shrank, and I was left to hang out with the kids who had a reputation for "getting into trouble". I wouldn't fit in there either. Eventually, I would become the target for them to bully, make fun of, and fight with. At times, when I saw these kids ahead on the road, I would take a long way home out of fear, I might catch a beating. Despite the fact these neighborhood thugs had their own insecurities, my insecurities were taking on a life of their own. Where did I fit in? I didn't fit in among the normal kids, and I certainly did not fit in among the abnormal. Having that feeling would be my introduction to my first experience with isolation; this idea was not by choice, but it was real.

It was also during this time period a neighbor of ours would take advantage of me in ways no adult should engage with a child. He had asked me to cut his lawn to earn some additional cash; for a young teenager, this was gold. But he had other goals in mind. He had a sickness I cannot identify with. Things like this are not uncommon, sadly. But for me, there was a lot of guilt and shame that I carried with me for decades. I had done nothing wrong; he was a sick man, a very sick man. I could have done away with years of guilt and shame if I had only told my parents what had happened. They would have comforted me and helped me deal with the situation. But as a young teenager, I wanted to bury my head in the sand so nobody could see me. I didn't even consider telling my parents.

Again, this would come down to me thinking my parents would think less of me. Nothing could have been further from the truth, but it is how I saw it then. Maybe I saw it that way because I blamed myself for allowing it to happen to me. Again it really wasn't my fault, but sometimes we blame ourselves even when there is no justification for the blame. This leads to self resentment.

My parents are good people, very loving people; they weren't intentionally neglectful and had their own stories. They did the best they could with the tools they had. But the end result, my experience growing up, was one of constant fear and having to lie in certain situations just to try and keep the peace. My parents were not always loyal to their vows, and my mom would take us kids with her from time to time when she visited her new "friend," Dad would inquire as to where mom had taken us. I would learn that lying avoided the pain and controversy that the truth would have resulted in. Another skill I would become very good at is lying. Throughout my childhood and adult life, I learned how to spin a story. I would never let the truth stand in the way of a good story. You couldn't tell it from looking at me, but I was torn up inside, confused, and scared all the time.

So when the opportunity came where I could be like the others through drinking and such, I was on board. In High School, the feeling of "less than" was magnified. I was very lazy when it came to my schoolwork, and my grades reflected that. So if you got good grades, and by good grades, I mean a "C," you intimidated me. I also was not very big in high school, so the basketball coach and the football coach were not chasing me down, even though I loved sports. So if you were athletic, you intimidated me. As I said we came from very modest means, my parents had five kids to feed, 5 kids to clothe, so we didn't get many new outfits to wear, so if you dressed nice in school, you intimidated me. If you walk around constantly feeling intimidated, your self esteem isn't very good, your confidence is nonexistent, so if you were a girl you intimidated me.

Don't get me wrong, I have a lot of good memories from this time period in school, but that was because of some of the people around me who tried to make me feel a part of things. They tried, and I pretended to feel accepted; the truth was I never really felt accepted despite the fact I probably was. One of those people was my friend John.

One day, John invited me to come hang out with him and some others. They were going to have a fire in the woods and party. He told me if I gave him some money, he would get me some alcohol for the party, so I did. I went to that fire that night and met my friend John. He gave me a bottle of Southern Comfort and introduced me to the others. The others welcomed me and offered me some of their alcohol. Once again, people were trying to make me feel welcome and feel part of it, but my insecurities wouldn't allow me to see this at the time. Regardless of everyone's efforts, I still felt less than others. As I drank that alcohol that night, the feeling of less than seemed to slip away.

I could talk to the athletes, the good students, and even the girls. They no longer intimidated me. Alcohol had eased that feeling. I believe at that moment, my brain registered that alcohol was a solution to that problem. So, I would begin my reliance on alcohol to solve my problems, or so I thought. These parties in the woods would become my escape, and I would become a regular attendee. I wasn't going for the people. I was going so I could drink and smoke pot.

I had discovered a new way to be able to exist, to feel comfortable with my situation and myself. I would start to seek out the partiers, the people who drank like I drank. Every weekend would consist of me getting someone of age to buy me my booze. It would, of course, have a price associated with it, like paying for their booze for them, but I was willing to do that. But as I look back on standing in the liquor store parking lots and soliciting strangers to take my money in the hope they would do the right thing. I see that was a dangerous thing to have done just for the sake of getting my alcohol. I would also experience a sense of worth when I had booze. The rest of the kids in my neighborhood would be my friends. It never occurred to me that they were just using me because I had the cheapest beer one could afford. During this time, I had a coveted paper route and, actually, for a teenager, made really decent money, the money I quickly disposed of through buying liquor and pot. My friends who had jobs spent their money on nicer things like designer jeans, the latest hit rock albums, concert tickets, and other things teenagers were so interested in. But I would continue to be okay with the hand-me-downs that made me feel less than as long as I could get drunk and escape the world.

As I got older, the parties became more sophisticated in many ways. First, I didn't have to drink in the woods, nor did I need someone to buy my booze. I was of legal age and could buy my own, go to clubs, and do all the other things adults do. Alcohol was becoming my best friend. I would always make sure it was part of my plans. I had even discovered through one of my uncles that other recreational drugs would intensify my escape from reality. I would convince myself this was normal, that everybody did what I was doing. The reality was not everyone looked to escape life. My childhood friends had grown up and had real jobs with real careers and futures. I still didn't know what I wanted to be when I grew up. Knowing I could be more than I had become was taking root. I battled myself every day for not being better. I would deal with these feelings by not feeling. Do you know who else goes on each day without feeling? The deceased, I was slowly dying inside.

I would bounce from a meaningless job to a meaningless job. I was working a couple of different jobs as I couldn't seem to secure a position that would pay me well enough to only have one job. One of those jobs was in a convenience store; the hours were flexible, the daily tasks pretty simple, and the people who came into the store were interesting, to say the least. But it would be at this job that my luck would turn a bit. I would meet a girl. She was pretty and seemed to be very put together. I was immediately attracted to her smile. She worked at the same store as I did; she did this part-time as she had a full-time job that she did well at. I would look at the store schedule and find her phone number. I went to her full-time job to ask her on a date. All of this is normal, right? Only if you're some creepy stalker, which I guess I was. She agreed to go to dinner with me, and we started to hang out and go on a couple of dates. I was enjoying myself; she was like an angel sent from heaven. If you only knew how much that turned out to be true. After a month of dating, I did what anyone would do. I proposed to her. Needless to say, she was taken off guard by this; who wouldn't be? She was smart, she agreed to take the ring but said she would think about the proposal. She did eventually agree to marry me.

Looking back on things, this was the best thing that could have ever happened to me. She has been by my side and been my rock since that day. I truly believe if it had not been for her and her guidance, I would not be here today.

Eventually, I would enter into world politics; this is not a good idea if you're an active alcoholic. Political campaigns are full of drinking events; some of them would offer open bars, and I would always make time for those.

Drinking is an accepted practice in the political world and a good excuse for the family members who questioned my drinking. Many great ideas would flow from people when they had a few in them. But politics is as tough emotionally as running a marathon is physically. I had dreams of changing the world and making an impact for the better. I didn't know how unrealistic an expectation that was; politics is as cutthroat as any business I know of. My skills as an alcoholic had prepared me well for this, though. Being able to change character midstream and pretend I actually cared about the most trivial things, all for the sake of being liked. I was a pro at spinning a story full of lies by now and breaking promises. All that practice was paying off.

The political world is full of illusions; what the outside public sees is not reality. Things are sometimes carefully staged and scripted behind closed doors to give the "audience" a show. Manipulation is an essential skill in politics; to get support for things you want or need, sacrifices must be made. It wasn't at all what I thought it would be. I was fascinated by the dream of doing good and helping the community. I thought we were all on the same team once the elections were done, but I was wrong. It was about self-preservation. Some had bigger political aspirations, and this seat was just a placeholder, a resume builder. It was a game, life was a game, and I needed to play the game.

But in all that, somewhere along the line, I lost myself. I don't know when that actually happened, but I had become void of feeling and ambition. My plans started to center around my drinking; nothing else seemed to matter. I really didn't know what I actually cared about. I mean, I loved my wife and my kids, but that's where my world ended. I didn't have any real friends; those who called themselves my friends were like me; they had alternative goals from that relationship. My maternal family had all but disappeared from my life. My sisters stayed close to each other, but I did not. I had always blamed my mom for this. That night when she had me grab my bag and go with my dad was the cause of it all, I thought. But that was a lie. I chose to be an outsider. That feeling of less than started to become my normal feeling.

I didn't know what I was supposed to be doing with my life; I just knew I wasn't doing it. As in my early teen years, my social circle was shrinking, but this time, it had nothing to do with my parents, nothing to do with my family. I was always in a state of self-pity; everyone had it out for me, I thought. Nothing ever went my way, I thought. Poor me, life isn't fair; Vodka would fix that.

By the time I was in my mid-thirties, my alcoholism had evolved with some other substances being added in; things that in my teens I had been exposed to but was easily able to walk away from, but would now, from time to time become part of my diet. They would never have a grip like my drinking did, but they would become more accepted in my mind.

Let's just say I have done a lot of different drugs in my time, mostly to enhance or chase the feeling I used to get from drinking alone. I had started to hide my drinking; I would drink openly around people, but that would be controlled. I didn't want anyone to see the real drinker I had become. That by itself should have told me something. I never hid anything I was proud of, only the things I was ashamed of. I had resorted to drinking in my car and my garage after everyone in the house was sleeping. I had resisted the urge to drink during the workday, but that was all I could control when it came to my drinking. I had developed a shield of egotism that became my go-to defense for my drinking in my head. We owned a home. My kids always had the best of what they needed. Bills were paid (thanks to my wife), and we had saved money in the bank, so surely I deserve the right to drink. But even though our position in life was good, I can't help but wonder today how much better it would have been if I wasn't so self-centered, if I was so dependent upon booze to deal with life's everyday events.

Then, the event that would lead to my last serious alcoholic run would happen. My father had been diagnosed with cancer, stage four cancer. Death was imminent for him. I quickly felt self-pity. My father was dying, but I felt sorry for myself and that I had to go through it. I had wasted so much time that I could have had with him. I loved my dad dearly; despite all that was in the past, he had sacrificed his own happiness for his kids. When my parents ultimately divorced and my mom would eventually move out of state, my father kept my sisters and me in our state, in our home. He was from Mississippi; his family still lived there. He had always wanted to move back home, but for his kids, he decided to stay in Rhode Island. That was the only home we really knew, and he would put us ahead of his own desires.

As I said, he was a good man and a loving man. My dad got sick in October 2004 and passed away on January 1, 2005.

During that time, I would visit my dad daily, then get drunk every night out of self-pity and guilt. The feelings were real to a certain extent, but in reality, it was my decisions that resulted in the lost time between my dad and me. I think deep down I was feeling angry at God for taking my dad from me before I could spend the time I should have with him. Alcohol was the only way I knew how to address those feelings, to not feel those feelings; again, alcohol was a solution to that problem.

I would watch my dad, a once strong and independent person, wither away into a skeleton. In the end, my dad was in a morphine coma, unable to speak; we would have to sit by his bed and watch him die.

While my dad was going through the final months of his life, my family saw I was hurting. They knew I was drinking, but because I was going through what I was going through, they did not address my drinking. To an alcoholic, this is akin to having permission to drink, and I would run with it. As alcoholics, we do those things. We take advantage of every situation that benefits our immediate wants, regardless of the real damage we are doing. I could never see the potential damage to myself or those involved. So, when my family was being compassionate to my pains, I was being selfish and going far beyond what I should have been doing. I would even become defensive if anyone even dared to ask me if I thought maybe I was drinking too much.

This would be the beginning of a ten-year downward spiral. I would push every barrier for the next ten years; at times, I knew I was drinking too much, but by this time, the drink was choosing me. I was showing up, but I wasn't there. Drinking during the day, during the night, whenever I could.

By this time, I had become very good at hiding my bottles and planning my drinking. I had reached the point where feelings were a luxury, and when I had them, I didn't want them, and Vodka would fix that. Being numb had become my comfort zone. I wasn't drinking for the purpose of being social; I was drinking so I could live, so I could deal with life, so I didn't feel. I was at a point where the only thing worth living for was my wife and my daughters. Everything else was scary.

As I said, it was around this time that my drink started choosing me. I don't know if you know what I actually mean by that; maybe it hasn't happened to you yet. But I was really at the point where I didn't want to drink anymore, or at least I wanted to get control over my drinking. I would set out to explore some controlled drinking. I would tell myself only a couple of beers but eventually end up drunk all over again. I was in sales and on the road a lot. Business meetings with a client would always involve a cocktail for lunch or dinner. The intent wasn't to get drunk but to drink socially. During this time, I wasn't aware that wasn't an option for me. All of those events would trigger the body allergy, and I couldn't stop once I started. I had truly lost the choice to drink or not drink.

In October 2005, 9 months after losing my dad, I started a business after losing a very good job as a result of a merger. Starting this company would require funding, money I didn't really have. With the support of my wife, and I always had her support, I went to a venture capital company to get that funding, but it would mean I would have to put everything we had on the line. My family's home and other assets would all be at risk. Venture capital loans are like legal loan sharking. My interest rate was extremely high. My interest payment alone would be $7,000. I would also need an office, office furniture, computers, and a few employees to get this started. All in all, I had about 17 months' worth of money to get this business cash-positive so I didn't lose everything I had and leave my family homeless. This was during my ten-year spiral, so I wasn't in the best space thinking-wise, but I would need to be, if I were to be successful. Oh, and just to remind you, I hadn't even finished High School. Only an alcoholic would think all this was a good idea.

The early days of this business were filled with hard work and even harder drinking. I had asked two of my business friends to join me in this venture. I chose them based on our partying times together, not based on what they actually had for business experience. I mean, they both were good salespeople, but the truth is I would be able to drink with them, and they wouldn't think anything of it as long as they got their paychecks. Once again, I was buying my friendships like I did in my teen years.

The smarter move here would have been to partner with my wife as she knew how to manage money and always seemed to have a good business mind. But she would have been critical of my spending and my drinking, so I would opt for the softer, easier approach. The daily thoughts of failure hung over me like a cloud during a thunderstorm; Vodka would be my umbrella. I would start to create a less-than-perfect home life for my family. Vodka would help me see why that was ok. Working late hours, coming home drunk, and being a complete ass to my wife because "she didn't understand," but I didn't give her the information so she could understand. But somehow, within the first year, I was cash-positive, not debt-free, but I could pay the bills.

I would go on to build a successful business; again, I wonder just how much more successful it would have been if I had been sober during this time. I don't think I had a sober day from the day my dad first got ill, and yet, somehow, I survived. But not unharmed. I was in a deep alcoholic depression on the inside. I no longer feared death and almost welcomed it. Some nights, when I crawled into bed totally drunk, I would think it would be okay if I didn't wake up the next day. But then, thoughts of my daughters and wife would come into my mind, and I would muster a desire to want to live. I never thought about taking my own life. I always saw that as the ultimate act of selfishness, but the flame of life I once had was down to a flicker.

I tried and tried again to break away from drinking, but no matter what I did, I couldn't stay away. Until that morning on June 24th, standing in front of that mirror, I did not recognize the person on the other side. I knew why I felt the way I did. I knew I would be incapable of keeping the promise I had just made in the shower. But in that moment of hopelessness, I would come up with a plan of what to do. Even though I would end up drinking that day, it was a truly miraculous day for this alcoholic. I can see that today. I couldn't on that day. Recovery is a wonderful thing.

Chapter 03

APPLYING THE STEPS TO MY LIFE

The Big Book of AA actually talks about all of the things and feelings I described in my story. First, where my brain saw alcohol as a solution to my problems would in itself become the problem. The Big Book explains that my problem centers on my mind rather than my body. My brain seeing alcohol as something that would relieve the pain, whether it be physical pain or emotional pain, would become my justification for my drinking.

Our brains process physical pain and emotional pain in the same way. To the brain, it's just pain. I would deal with that pain by not feeling at all; I had been self-medicating. I used the events of my past to be the foundation of each day of the present. Things that had been done decades in the past were as real for me each day as though they were happening now. My mind had created an alternative existence that allowed me to feel justified in my thinking. But was I really justified?

The fact that others were born with different bodies and were more athletic than I was wasn't unique to just me; it's how I saw it and how I processed it, that was the issue. I was healthy, I played recreational sports, I just wasn't good enough, big enough to play for my high school team. The reality is by the time I reached High School, I already had low self-esteem, I didn't believe in myself, and liquor always took those feelings away for a short period of time.

The program of recovery convinces me that my disease lives in my mind rather than my body. Yes, it is true that I could not stop drinking once I started. I never planned to get drunk, just have a couple drinks but I could never stop after starting and that was a result of what is referred to as my body's allergy to alcohol. Yeah, I heard that gasp of, "Well, that sounds stupid." How can anyone who drinks as much as I do have an allergy to alcohol? That is a perfectly normal response. It was my response as well. I thought I knew what an allergy was. I didn't get a runny nose, sneeze, or break out in a rash when I drank. I knew those were all things that happened if you had an allergy to something. I once asked my sponsor, Dean, when I was early in sobriety what do I say if someone asked me why I didn't drink anymore. His response? Tell them you're allergic to alcohol. At the time, that was the most insane thing I had ever heard. How could anyone who drinks as much as I do possibly have an allergy to alcohol?

Well, I would learn the answer to that question while trying to prove it wrong. First, I would need to understand what an allergy actually was. I would go to the American Academy of Allergy Asthma & Immunology to learn more. I would find the definition of an allergy to be "An allergy is a chronic condition involving an abnormal reaction to an ordinarily harmless substance."

That made sense to me. I know others can drink normally, controlling their intake and not needing to get drunk every time. I could certainly see how others may see my actions when I drank as being abnormal, but how is that an allergy? I would learn that my body actually reacts differently in the way it metabolizes alcohol. I don't want to sound overly scientific here, as I am not that smart. However, I came across a study in a medical journal published in 1979 that would explain the process by which alcohol is absorbed by the body. When a non-alcoholic drinks alcohol, their body takes the ethanol in alcohol and has enzymes in their body that convert that to acetaldehyde, which is itself a toxin, then other enzymes convert that to diacetic acid, then to acetate, and finally to water, carbon dioxide, and sugar. The water is expelled from the body through the urinary tract, the carbon dioxide through the respiratory system, and the sugar is burned through physical activity.

Now, when it comes to the body of the alcoholic, everything is the same, except when we get to the acetate phase. It seems an alcoholic doesn't have the proper enzymes to convert the acetate. Now, the organs that produce those enzymes are the pancreas and the liver; which we all know are the organs alcohol attacks first. Our pancreas and liver can be healthy in every other aspect except the ability to generate those enzymes in either the proper quantity or quality. That acetate takes longer to metabolize. Science has also discovered that if that acetate remains in our system for a time frame longer than it should, it creates a craving for the same substance that created the acetate.

For me, that was great news. It explained why I always had to have another drink once I started, or when I had already had more than enough. It explained to me why I always seemed to crave a drink at the end of the night more than I did at the beginning. It explained that even though I truly only wanted one or two beers in the past, I couldn't stop once I started. I wasn't morally broken. I wasn't a mental defect.

The manifestation of my allergy is in the phenomenon of craving, not itchy eyes or sneezing. This, for me, made sense, and it was a welcome relief. Now, the medical world has no cure for this, and if I put a drink in my body today, that same process will happen. AA does not address the body allergy as there is no cure for this. It focuses on the fact my disease centers in my mind.

My perception of life and all its people was the main part of my problem. I had been programming myself that the only way I could feel better was to not feel, and drinking did that for me. Rather than looking at the problem of how I saw things, how I felt about things, and accepting those feelings and working through them, instead I drank. After all, my feelings and perceptions all live in my mind, not in my body. Anger comes from my thoughts, fear from my thoughts, love from my thoughts. I would need to look at that, and that is what the program of Alcoholics Anonymous would help me do.

I mentioned in my opening that Step 1 was admitting I was powerless over alcohol and that my life had become unmanageable. So what exactly does that mean?

Well, I just looked at what happens when I put a drink in my body; my body lets me know it cannot handle it and requires more and more. So, for me, I cannot drink in safety. I had been seeing alcohol as a fixer of all things. I had been programming myself that alcohol was my go-to, in bad times and in good. The mind is a powerful and amazing thing. It processes information and retains information so it can help the body survive. Throw a rubber ball at a very young child (don't do this), and it will bounce off them. But throw a ball at an older kid or an adult, and they will either move out of the way or catch it. All without the need to sit down and figure out what to do. Because the mind has already registered what they do if an object is thrown their way.

The mind can also determine the potential danger of an object or a situation, and the pain it may bring. All my life, my mind saw alcohol as an answer, not a problem. So when problems came up, my reflex, my thoughts went straight to booze to solve them. We do so many things today seemingly without thought, but the reality is our brain is thinking and responding so quickly we do not realize we actually have the thought. So those harmless early-day drinking bouts were actually supplying my mind with the data it needed to survive, to not feel pain. That would be fine if my body was not alcoholic, but my body is. So, if I cannot stop thinking about drinking, and I cannot stop drinking once I start, I am, in fact, powerless over alcohol.

The unmanageability part actually comes from within. When we cannot figure out why we are doing some of the crazy stuff we do. I failed to understand that I was building my life on a bed of quicksand. I was not able to deal with my feelings, always feeling insecure, feelings of impending doom, and all the guilt and shame you can imagine. That is the unmanageability in my life. These feelings are actually a fire feeding itself fuel, or what I read in a book, a feedback loop from hell. The worse I felt about myself would make me feel even worse about feeling worse. It was never about the hurt relationships, the lost jobs, the jail stays. Those things happen to non-alcoholics, too. It was not knowing how to live in my own skin.

A lot of alcoholics take the external events in their life as what they see as unmanageable. I get that it is easy to see the results externally but not so easy to recognize the internal struggle. People feel because they drink and have a problem with drinking, their families have forever written them off. I do not see it that way.

What is probably closer to the truth is our families stand by us as long as they can. Time after time, we go back to our life of addiction, and they get disappointed and hurt. Our families love us; they want to see us have a happy life. When we raise their hopes time and time again only to have that hope smashed, they feel pain. But that pain is for us, for our struggles they see us going through. Eventually, they make a decision not to be part of that pain. After all, most of us have put great effort into pushing them away to start. I have seen families reunited once the alcoholic becomes sober and regains their will to live.

Many feel they need to have their jobs and their families back before they can jump into getting sober. The opposite is the real truth here; we must first work on ourselves to be able to have those things back in our lives. We will not need to work on those things as they will come naturally as we improve our own situation by working on ourselves first. We have lived a life of sheltering ourselves from daily living for a while. We had stopped growing, so in that sense, we stopped living.

My unmanageability began at a young age when things in my house confused the hell out of me. I wasn't comfortable enough or confident enough to have conversations with people so I could understand what I was feeling. I shouldn't have understood all the things going on; I was too young, but I also didn't know where to turn for answers. In my house, feelings were personal and should be kept to oneself. Maybe it was because my parents didn't know how to handle their own feelings, or maybe it was just another wrong perception on my part. Either way, I was never exposed to how to deal with my feelings.

I was not equipped to deal with what life would send my way, and when I didn't know how to handle it, I would numb those feelings with alcohol. The truth is I stopped growing emotionally, socially, and spiritually when I started to rely on alcohol. There was no further need to learn. My booze was my encyclopedia to life. Then, when we realize that our drinking is at least a part of the problem and we cannot stop when we want to, we get torn up inside, making us feel even worse. We see others able to take it or leave it; why can't we? I used to be able to control my drinking but had lost that ability; why? We are now actually battling with ourselves. There is no winner when you battle yourself.

Those feelings of less than, feelings we are letting others down, that depression and feelings of never-ending doom, that's the real unmanageability. How we see ourselves and feel about ourselves. Because we don't really know or understand ourselves anymore. The fact for me is I didn't want to look at myself; it was scary, so I thought.

After all, I was a victim for all my life. Now, I would need to look at the truth, the facts, the reality. That truth that reality would be that only I saw myself as a victim, and I would build that into a self-fulfilling prophecy. In certain situations, I may have been a victim, like when my neighbor made me a victim. But as for the rest, being a victim was convenient, and best of all, it gave me my reasons for drinking. I certainly wasn't the victim in my parent's relationship; sure, it wasn't the best of childhoods, but I wasn't the victim. My mom was a victim; my dad was a victim. I was just unintended collateral damage. There was never any intent from my parents to cause their kids harm; it just happened to be the result of reality.

When I got to Step 2, it presented an entirely different set of issues for me. I had grown up in a catholic family, made all my sacraments, and actually believed in a higher power, a God. My issues here were different from some of the people I had spoken to when I came to AA, different but the same in some ways. I didn't know who or what God really was. I was told who God was, but I was also told who Santa Claus was and who The Easter Bunny was. That turned out to be a big lie. I could get on board with some of the things I had heard in church but had some reservations about others. I was what the Big Book refers to as agnostic. Being agnostic simply means a person who neither believes nor disbelieves in a god or religion. For me, I believed there was a power that created life and the world we live in. I just didn't necessarily believe everything I was told about God, so I dismissed it all. I was also in a bad place, a place that was based on my decisions and the way things were in my life, my feelings, and my victimization. I was left to wonder why God would let this happen to me. Those feelings were really just another example of playing the victim.

God wasn't responsible for my situation; I was. I was actually being a coward for not taking that responsibility and blaming Him for my decisions. God wasn't responsible for my alcoholism. I was. I don't know about you, but God never once came down and bought me a drink at the bar. Again, fear would be part of my problem. I have always associated God with Death. My church, my religion, was about dying to be with God. Eternal life through death is terrifying to me. But today, I know that of all God's creatures, we humans are the only ones who think about death; the rest of His creations just live each day.

Of all the species on earth, we humans seem to be the only species that have the gift of free will. Only humans can have a thought and then have a thought about their thought. The rest of God's creatures don't. Only humans can have sex for the sake of having sex. Other animals don't have that luxury; they have sex for the simple purpose of reproducing. So God was not responsible for anything that had happened to me nor why I was alcoholic; if I were to find blame with God, it would have to be that he gave me free will, that he allowed me to make my own decisions and that's just silly, as that is a gift.

God can best be explained to me by an Albert Einstein quote. "Evil does not exist, sir, or at least it does not exist unto itself. Evil is simply the absence of God. It is just like darkness and cold, a word that man has created to describe the absence of God. God did not create evil. Evil is not like faith or love that exists, just as light and heat. Evil is the result of what happens when a man does not have God's love present in his heart. It's like the cold that comes when there is no heat or the darkness that comes when there is no light."

The evil in my life was created by the decisions I made and the thinking I used to make them. There can be no bad without the existence of good. I could believe this; from that simple willingness to believe, I could begin to build the life of good that I have today. After all, I did believe in God when it was convenient for me. I think we've all prayed to God to get us out of some mess we found ourselves in. I know I have. I have promised if He got me out of a situation, I would never do it again, only to do it again and again.

I didn't need to know who or what God was, nor what God looked like; I simply needed to know I was not God, and I was already certain of that. I can't make a tree, a flower. I am not capable of creating everything in this world that I enjoy daily. It also answers the age-old question: What came first, the chicken or the egg? You cannot have one without the other, so life had to begin somewhere, and if that was by the hand of some Power of the Universe, that would make sense, wouldn't it? Besides, do you really need to be convinced that there is a power greater than you? In Step 1, you admitted you were powerless over alcohol, thus admitting there was a Power greater than you. Alcohol was my God, and I needed a better God.

Besides, as I previously mentioned, sanity is the ability to see the truth from the false. I had grown up all my life knowing that alcohol created problems. In addition to what went on in my household, I had plenty of other relatives who would show me what happens with heavy drinking. Every summer in August, we would have a family cookout. August was not only my birthday, but I shared that day with an uncle and every year, there would be a cookout at his home. Year after year, I would see my aunts and uncles drink, and chaos always erupted by the end of the night. Fists flying, arguments going on, all among family members who, when they were not drinking, were very loving people. I had ignored the truth as I witnessed it and had only relied on how I felt when drinking. I was not capable of seeing the truth from the false anymore.

Before I move on to the next step, I want to circle back to what I just wrote above. I want to discuss the word willingness. This may be one of the most overlooked words in sobriety, but also one of the most important words. One has to ask themselves, what lengths am I willing to go to so I can become sober and improve my life? If you have a problem answering that question, try this one: What were you willing to do for your drink or your drug? What were you willing to sacrifice for your alcohol? Who were you willing to disappoint to protect your "right" to get drunk? If you do not have the willingness to toss aside any prejudices and be open to new ideas, you may as well close the book now and throw it in the trash can because you are not ready to live sober.

Before I got sober, my life sucked donkey balls. It really didn't, but that was my perception of my life before I got sober. If I were to improve upon that, change would be required. This isn't an all-you-can-eat lunch buffet where you take what you want and leave the rest behind. This is more of a healthy diet where you get what you need. If I knew what I needed, I wouldn't have needed AA. Yet there were millions and millions of people just like me who had found a better life through this miraculous program. While I was living a life of isolation and misery. It is as simple as one of my AA friends, Tony, puts it; "It's as simple as baking a cake."

If you want the cake to come out right, you need to follow the directions on the box. If it calls for two eggs and you add three, it won't come out the way it is supposed to. If it says to bake at three hundred and fifty degrees for twenty minutes and you bake it at four hundred for five minutes, it won't come out the way it should. Are you willing to try things that you do not understand yet? Are you willing to see your best thinking got you where you are today? Are you willing to follow some directions and see just how good the cake can be? If you are, that is a major part of the battle, and your odds of success just got much better. If you're not willing to explore what your life can be like, you need to ask yourself what you are afraid of.

Fear of the unknown is what holds us back and stops us from growing. In the days of Christopher Columbus, people thought the world was flat and feared sailing off the edge of the world if they ventured too far. But Columbus thought he could get east by sailing west. He would face the fears of his time and set out west, and now we know the world is round. I can assure you if you overcome your fears of what life will be like without your drug or drink, you will not sail off the edge of the world, but you must be willing to set aside what you think it will be like so you can discover what your world can look like.

Step 3 is the first step to use the word decision in it. But the first three steps of recovery are all decision steps. That is what makes this program so simple. How It Works, or Chapter 5 of the Big Book, emphasizes the need to be honest. But it doesn't speak to being honest with others. It speaks about being honest with ourselves. After all, how can I expect to be honest with anyone else if I can't be honest with myself? If we are ready to be honest and see things for what they really are, then we are ready to make some decisions.

First, in order to admit I am powerless in step 1, I must first make the decision that I am powerless based on the facts. For me, I have already described the real facts. I couldn't control how much I would drink, and when I wanted to stop, I couldn't stay away from a drink. If I drink even when I don't want to, and if I am unable to control exactly how much I drink, am I willing to be honest enough to admit that to myself? Can I see that I have no power over alcohol? I also am left to decide if my life is manageable or unmanageable based on the facts. Again, here, I had plenty of evidence, but I was never willing to actually look at it or acknowledge it. When someone doesn't even feel comfortable in their own skin, is their life really manageable? Is it manageable to be fighting with yourself every day? My desire to not drink was there, but my inner feelings towards myself required that I drink. For a very long time, I hadn't been able to manage my life. Sure, on the outside, it looked great, but inside was where the unmanageability lived. Was I ready to admit it?

In step two, I have to decide if I can return to a sane way of life and if I am capable of doing that on my own or if I can use some help. I had relied on my successes to shield me from looking at this sanity thing. I had a successful business. I employed over a dozen people. I made good money and had nice things. Insane people don't have what I have. That was my thinking. But it was about my sanity around taking the first drink that I needed to look at. By now, I could look at the past and see what drinking had done to me rather than for me. Drinking had overcome all reasonable thinking in my life. When the day was young, and I was suffering from my drinking the night before, I knew I had to stop. But as the day progressed, I would convince myself that it wasn't that bad. I wasn't able to remember the feelings from earlier in the day. Sanity here simply is losing sight of the truth when it comes to my drinking, nothing else. Both of those decisions in steps one and two need to be actually made by looking at things.

It's not; let's check the box because we've discussed it. If I am not truly convinced of the need to make the first two decisions, my third decision will not be built on a solid foundation and will collapse. Ask yourself, can you control your drinking? Are you able to stop when you want without going back to it? Are you comfortable in your own skin? Do you seek isolation? Do you only hang out with people who drink like you do? Do you consider your life to be manageable to the point you are comfortable with everything you do and the way you act? Have you ever forgotten the promises you've made to yourself or made excuses to have that drink?

If you can look at those two decisions and honestly answer them, you've made a start. The Big Book spends close to 70 pages trying to help us answer the first two questions because the third question, the third step, is crucial to understand and accept before going on to the fourth step.

Many alcoholics have a problem at Step 3, a problem making a decision to trust in a power they are not aware of. We constantly rely on visual evidence, but visual evidence is the weakest of all. When I walk into a room and flip a light switch on, I simply see the lights come on. But the electricity that travels through the wires to power the light is unseen, but it is there. What visual evidence was there that said a man could fly? Yet two brothers who owned a bicycle repair shop believed we could achieve flight when everyone else had given up on the idea and they achieved the impossible. Visual evidence is all around us as to a power greater than human power, but for some reason, we have a problem with the concept.

But if you do believe that there is a power out there that can help restore your sanity, wouldn't you be eager to let Him help? As an alcoholic, I didn't ever need nor want anyone's help most of my life. I saw it as a weakness. So, if I was to turn anything over, to have faith and trust anyone else, I certainly needed to start by being willing to believe.

Besides, I hadn't been doing such a great job of things on my own at this point. After all, I was in AA, which was never a lifelong ambition of mine, but that's where I landed running the show on my own. So, what did I have to lose? So, exactly what am I turning over? My worries, my fears, just to name the top two. I would need to trust that my Higher Power has a plan for me, and I need to simply stop fighting it. Am I more powerful than a God? No. So why fight? It was actually a relief for me when I made this decision.

By turning my Will over, I would change my thinking. My thoughts would not be driven by fear anymore. I would trust in my higher power that things would work out regardless of how they looked at that moment. Making my decisions based on fears hadn't really worked out for me historically. If my thoughts were God-conscious, then my actions would reflect those thoughts. That may sound like a bunch of holy garbage to some, but let me ask you this. Is it garbage to be considerate of others' thoughts and feelings? Is it garbage, to be honest, so others know how we feel? Is it garbage to want to live a life of honesty so we can help others while helping ourselves? Is it garbage to not be looking over our shoulder, afraid of what is coming up behind us? Because that is the alternative.

That's what my life used to be like. I am going to die one day; that is a fact. Should I live my life in fear until that day comes, or should I enjoy each day and actually live the life I was intended to live? I choose to live in today, not yesterday. I choose to let someone else pilot my journey so I can enjoy the scenery. Does that sound so horrible? I didn't think it did.

Besides growing up in that neighborhood, I had friends who not only went to church but honestly believed in God. They didn't lecture anyone about God; they were not overly religious, but they believed in a God. But I saw they lived a way of life much different than I did. They thought of others. They were nice people who did nice things. In fact, I have been acquainted with lots of people who lived the same way. Their lives seemed to be happy; they were always seemingly at peace. Even at times I couldn't understand them not being mad at the world.

Church people are not perfect; nobody is. It's not about going to church; it's not particularly about religion. It's about not judging a group of people based on the actions of one or a small group of a much larger group. It's about looking at the miracle of life and how it could have possibly come to be without some Higher Power in play. When you meet a person who has faith who has spirituality, you meet a person who has God in their life. It is not about religion; for me, it is about spirituality and the peace of mind one enjoys when they are spiritually healthy.

When you make a decision, it is based on options. My options were to go on until the bitter end or be willing to go down a different road, one that I was the copilot. Because, as the pilot, I was constantly lost, frustrated, and angry. I was very willing to be rid of those feelings, and if that meant trying something different, I was ready. It stands to reason that I can't have a different life if I don't change the way I handle my life, a simple concept but hard to do.

The Spiritual Experience mentioned so many times in the Big Book is explained on page 567 of the Big Book.

The explanation is simple, really; it describes a Spiritual Experience as being a personality change sufficient enough to bring about recovery from alcoholism; every word in that appendix references change. Google "Spiritual Experience in the Big Book" and read it. You will see words like alteration, transformation, upheaval, and change. All those words mean the same thing: change. If I take the first word we spoke of, "willingness," and include that with the meaning of a Spiritual Experience, I get the willingness to change. I would certainly need a power greater than I to accomplish that.

I already had plenty of history, plenty of evidence that my way of living life and my way of thinking never worked well for me, and that's exactly why I should be willing to turn things over. This goes beyond my childhood being what it was. If it was just the fact that my parents were to blame because they controlled things when I was young, then when I got older and I took control, things should have gotten better, but they didn't. In High School, at one of the parties in the woods, I had come to love so much that I would get a girl pregnant. Drinking had lowered my inhibitions. I didn't think of what the outcome could be. I didn't care. I was drunk, she was drunk, and we would sneak off into the woods, and she would end up pregnant. This is the part of my podium story where I talk about partying as more fun than studying. Now, my drinking would impact not only my life but also the lives of two others. There is no better definition or example of selfishness; my drinking now laid out the future of two other humans through my actions.

I would continue to make bad decisions throughout my life based on self-needs and wants, always influenced by my alcoholic thinking. Over time, I would be involved in two car accidents while I was drinking. The first one, I would ask a childhood friend to say he was driving. We had just left a liquor store to replenish our night supply, and for the record, he wasn't of legal drinking age. I had already been drinking that night when I hit a car pulling out of a parking lot. Oh, and I was in my uncle's truck that he loaned me. Beer was everywhere, and the cops were sure to check to see if anyone was drunk. So, I convinced my friend to take the fall. Not considering what that outcome would look like, not concerned as to how that would impact his future.

Well, what it looked like was his license being suspended and being responsible for ten thousand dollars in damages because, of course, neither of us had insurance. I would eventually own up and get my friend off the hook after months of him having to deal with the fallout, and I could now because the cops couldn't check me for being drunk.

That's just two examples of my thinking when I was drinking, but there are many more. I am quite certain you have your own. Just in those two stories, I had a negative impact on three people; that was only the tip of the iceberg in those stories. Those two stories would actually impact so many others. The reality for me when I looked at this was, I had been rationalizing my behaviors and my decisions. Rationalization by definition is giving a socially acceptable reason for socially unacceptable behavior, which is a form of insanity.

It's like tossing a stone in a pond and watching the ripples spread out. When I got that girl pregnant, I would impact her family. They would need to care for her during her pregnancy and help with the baby when he came. My friend's family would need to taxi him around while his license was suspended. There were more than just three people impacted by my actions and decisions. And clearly, this wasn't what my parents were doing. It was my own. Based on my own decisions, not theirs. So what harm could there be in turning my thinking over to God? He couldn't possibly do a worse job than I had been doing up until this point. And by this point, I mean I was 51 years old when I finally was able to come to this conclusion.

But looking back on it, God has always had my back. I should be dead at least three times over. Once, when I was just four years old, I was driving home with my dad. Back in those days, your parents' right arm was your seatbelt. We lived in Mississippi, and my dad was driving us home from his parents' house. He had been drinking. I was standing in the front seat, he lost control of his car, and we struck a tree. I was thrown through the windshield of the car. My forehead would be busted open, requiring seventy-two stitches to close, but I lived. I was four years old, head first through the windshield, and I lived.

When I was young we would move to Rhode Island. They were building a new home across from where I lived. I was 10 years old and curious. I went over to inspect the new foundation and wanted to go inside, but the bulkhead was locked. I decided I would climb in, but as I did, my jacket got snagged on something at the top of the foundation, and I was hanging, choking as my jacket acted like a noose. From out of nowhere, a man pulled me up. He saved me. He was passing by the house and had seen me climbing in. He saw what had happened and rescued me. We lived on a dead end; we didn't get much traffic on that road, but he was there to save me. I never saw him before that day nor after that day.

When I was in my forties and to make myself feel better, I bought a used boat despite the fact that I had never owned a boat or driven a boat. I decided I would take it on a maiden voyage. I had my business partner, two of my daughters, and my nephew with me. The engine of that boat would blow up directly under my feet, the cabin windows would be blown out, and the engine would be completely engulfed in flames. My youngest daughter would receive minor burns, and I would have burns from head to foot. My legs seriously hurt and blistered, skin hung from my hands and arms. My middle daughter would be traumatized when she saw her father in that condition as I made my way to the bow to check on her. Everyone on the boat would survive, I would survive, my burns would fully heal, and I would live. I was not drinking or drunk in any of those situations. All could have resulted in death, yet none did.

I believe God was always with me, whether I acknowledged that or not. It would only be when I got to Step 3 I could see it for the first time. It was God's will that I lived. It was not his will that I was in any of those scenarios. It was my dad's free will to drive drunk that night, my will to stand in the front seat. It was my free will to climb into an empty foundation for what? I don't know. It was my free will to buy a boat and decide to take it out with my family despite the fact I had never driven a boat before. To survive, all this and more had to be the result of loving power, and for me, that is God.

Step 4 required courage, as I had never experienced before. Because this step would require me to be 100% honest. It would also require me to be brave and not hide behind the fears that always stopped me from looking at the truth of things. This is not a typical trait of an alcoholic and a foreign language to me. Alcoholics are smart; they need to be to get away with what we get away with. But honesty was not something I had experience with. The honesty part, as well as the not caring what others thought of the real me part. But this is the step where the rubber hits the road. It is not a step to fear, as most do. There is nothing about this step you don't already know; in fact, some of this stuff enables your drinking.

What is very different about the Big Book of Alcoholics Anonymous and this book is I am not going to try and soft sell you. If your feelings get hurt, maybe you should ask yourself why. If the tone is too in your face, it's because I don't want you to die. When the Big Book was written, its intention was to let the reader know they were dealing with a life-or-death scenario, and they were. But it was also before the time alcoholism was recognized as a disease. At the time, some felt some of the words used in the Big Book were too harsh and softened the message a bit. This is why I haven't entered into writing this book with anyone else. You see, my sobriety has taught me I will always be an alcoholic, but I don't have to die from alcoholism, and neither do you. In order for me to keep my sobriety, I must live in a way that embraces honesty. They say sometimes the truth hurts. Looking at my life, I say that lies, lying to myself, and lying to you will bring far more pain than the truth could ever bring. It is my job to tell you the truth; what you do with it is yours.

This step, the 4th step, is the foundation for the remaining steps in recovery; skimp here, and you risk relapse. The reality is all we do here is take an inventory and figure out what we have been holding onto that causes us to rely on a drink. The step itself is simple; as I said, you already have the information to complete it. Plus, we are all very good when it comes to taking other people's inventory, so it's not something we have to learn how to do. In AA today, we have worksheets that make the process even easier. The only requirement is that we be willing to be honest and thorough as we complete them.

When I was a member of my first AA homegroup, "Age Doesn't Matter," I got to hear some others' experiences with this process. We were a commitment group, which meant we would go to other groups, and some of us would share our experiences with that group, and other groups would come to our meeting to share theirs. At one of our meetings, a visiting group came in, and one of the speakers, Bobby B, talked about the 4th step. Now, for context, I had been working on the 4th step at the time, so I was very interested in what he had to say. Bobby had been sober for quite some time, decades, and had been sponsoring men through the steps. I had my own sponsor, a very good sponsor who had been kicking me in the butt to complete this step because I had stalled.

But that night, when Bobby spoke, he didn't talk about the actual step. He spoke about his experience as a sponsor with the step. Bobby told how seventy-five percent of the guys he sponsored never started this vital step, and they all would relapse. Then he spoke about how some would start the step and not finish it, and the percentage of them that relapsed was shocking as well. Then he told about those who finished the step and how the vast majority of them were still in the program today and sober.

The timing of this message was impeccable. As I said, I had stalled in the completion of my own 4th step. Hearing Bobby that night was all I needed; as my friend Jamie says, "It takes a village." My sponsor was great; his name is Dean. He had been everything I had needed in a sponsor to this point and still is today. But sometimes, in recovery, we need to hear the same message from others to actually get the message; that's why it takes a village.

The fourth step is a crucial step in the recovery process. But it is also one that is easy to stall on. As you work through this step, you start to see some things about yourself. I started to see things about myself. As I saw these things, my alcoholic mind thought it saw the answers. So, I guess I didn't see much urgency in completing it. But the truth is I could only see what I was capable of seeing. It was more than I was aware of, so I thought I found the secret sauce. This is where a lot of alcoholics get tripped up. Where a lot stall and never finish. This had been the mistake that Bobby's sponsees had made; ego had gotten the better of them. They thought they knew all they needed to know. But the Big Book tells us self knowledge is not the answer.

After hearing Bobby speak that night and truly understanding his experience with his own sponsees, I got back to work on my 4th step the next day and finished it in two days. We have three worksheets to help us today with this step; they didn't have these in the very early days of AA; they wrote everything out longhand, so you're welcome.

The first sheet is the Resentment sheet. Before you dive into this, it is important to understand what a resentment actually is. The word resentment has a special meaning here. "Re" means to repeat something, like repaint, rework, or redo. The second part of the word "sentment" comes from the Latin word "sentire," which means to feel. So, the word resentment simply means to re-feel. A lot of people today in AA overuse this word, maybe because they don't know what it means. If I get annoyed at someone, then I am annoyed. I don't have a resentment. I can only have a resentment if you did something to me some time ago, and I continue to have those feelings over and over again.

When I came into AA, I was still angry over the fact that when my parents split up, my mother had me grab my bags, leave with my father, and go stay in a hotel. The fact I never let that go and felt the pain over and over that was a resentment. Years and years passed, but I still hung on to that memory and nurtured it in my alcoholic mind. When it first happened, it was my mother's fault, but reliving the pain over and over was my own doing, not hers. I doubt she even remembers the event. When I came into AA, I was still angry with my dad for the nights he hit my mom, forcing me to climb out the window and call the cops. Every time I had to do that, it was my dad's fault. The fact it still haunted me thirty-plus years later was mine. As I've said, my dad passed away in 2005, he was long gone, but I still held onto the pain.

But these and many other things I held onto that is what justified my drinking. "If you had my life, you'd drink too." Bullshit! Alcoholics see their personal problems as being unique; that's just not true. Many people have been through some of the same problems we have been through, more difficult problems than we've been through, and do not need to drink to fix their problems. It is how I felt about these things, how I nurtured these things. I have already explained how feelings live in the mind and my disease centers in my mind. Are we connecting the dots yet? Our goal here is to look at how and why we think about the past and why it is so important today. There are some legitimate reasons for originally having some of those feelings, but are they worth holding onto today? Are they true today?

The resentment sheet has four columns that need to be completed in preparation for your remaining steps.

Once again, the instructions for this worksheet are in the Big Book; it tells us exactly what we need to do step by step. It's like buying an entertainment center from Ikea. If you follow the directions, the product will come out the way it is supposed to. I am not going to explain each individual instruction point in the writing of the fourth step. I have my way of doing this, which may not look like another sponsor's way of doing it. So, in the spirit of not wishing to create unnecessary confusion, I'm simply going to give an overview here.

The Big Book instructs me to list all the people, institutions, and principles I am angry with. This doesn't mean I have to be angry in the moment; what this means is anger from the past as well as the present. For me, I would go through this using a timeline in my head. Where I lived at 8 years old, who I hung out with, sports or activities I did, teachers I had, etc., etc., I would repeat that in five-year intervals. I was amazed at some of the things I actually remembered, the people I remembered. As I thought about things, I would recall certain situations that made me feel less than others, and I would write down the people involved. I honestly didn't feel I was angry at anyone; as it turns out, I was angry at everyone.

The next instruction was to list why we were angry; for me, that was easy. I mean, they were on my list; I just needed to put down why they were there. This isn't done by writing intimate details but rather by using bullet points to help me remember what I need to discuss when I get to the 5th step.

The third column or third instruction would start to show me something. It deals with how what they did actually impacted me. We are all born with basic instincts of life.

First, we all have a Social Instinct that includes Companionship, Prestige, Self-esteem, Pride, Personal Relationships, and Ambitions. As humans, we are a social species. Things like relationships are important to everyone, not just alcoholics. Relationships can be carefully aligned with companionship and the things when healthy, help our self esteem.

Then, we have a Security Instinct that deals with Material things, Emotional Security, and our Ambitions. Feeling safe is important. Feeling secure financially is important to us, and feeling loved by others is important to us.

Finally, our Sex Instinct covers our acceptable sex acts, hidden sex lives, and the sort.

I would see it wasn't the person I was angry with; it was what they did in the second column. If anyone did the same thing, I would be mad at them also. So it was what they did rather than who did it. Then, I would look in the third column and see what they did to threaten my relationships, my finances, or my future plans.

So now, I saw, it wasn't the actual act of what was done; if anybody did anything to threaten those basic instincts, I would be mad. The simple truth is you can't get mad or upset without one of your basic instincts of life being threatened.

Everybody has these basic instincts of life; what was different for me was how I handled each of those situations and processed them all.

Most people address the situation when it is in front of them through honest and, yes, sometimes uncomfortable conversations, but not me. I would pretend to be one thing on the outside while pressing my real feelings deep down inside. I lacked the comfort in my own skin to have a normal conversation. Even if that conversation would have been painful, it would have been done and dealt with. I always saw the worst-case scenario, worried about what you would think about me for even having the conversation. Instead, my mind saw that as an unresolved issue. This gets back to the power of the mind. I didn't think about some of the things on this list all the time, not consciously, but my mind had neatly packed them away for use in the future.

The fact my mother left me and my sisters definitely impacted my social instinct through impacting my personal relationships. It definitely impacted my ambitions or future plans, my self-esteem, and my pride. I always saw our family being together despite my parents seemingly never being happy together. I was embarrassed my family was broken, even though it was never really unified.

The fact that my dad used to hit my mom also impacted my social instincts for all the reasons listed relating to my mom. But it also impacted my security instinct. I did not feel safe while this was going on. It definitely impacted my emotional security; I was afraid of my mom getting seriously hurt or what would become inevitable, them divorcing.

All these years, I thought it was them, but really, it was the way I couldn't see the truth. I couldn't see that scared little boy in my fifty-year-old body, but he was there. With the same self-esteem issues, the disgust that my ambitions for my family had been shattered and it was my parent's fault. That, too, would be a lie.

When I was done checking some boxes in the third column and looking to see where maybe I was responsible for this resentment. I may have had no responsibility when the act of each resentment started, but did I now?

The next column will show me my role. I would look and ask if I had been inconsiderate, selfish, dishonest, or self-centered and did I have any fears related to these things? Staying with Mom and Dad (I am sure they appreciate this), I went through and honestly looked to see if I had any blame involved in these resentments. It was not my fault my dad got physical with my mom. But all these years, I wasn't being considerate that he had been suffering through his own drinking. The fact he never drank until after his navy days, after he received third-degree burns over ninety percent of his body. He had to live with that pain; he was ashamed of his physical appearance. None of that was ever a consideration from my side, so yes, I had definitely been inconsiderate.

Had I been selfish and self-centered, you betcha. Sure, I feared for my mom's safety, but I always talked about my lost sleep, my need to crawl out the window, and my shame with the neighbors. I had only thought of myself, so yes, I had been self-centered.

Did I have the fear that carried this resentment forward, the fear that drove my decisions here? Yes, and not only while it was happening. I feared ever talking to my parents about this, even decades after the fact. I feared it would hurt them or, more selfishly, hurt my standing with them. So, this resentment was not my responsibility in the beginning, but the fact it was still alive, I had some role in that.

My parents' splitting and my mom's leaving were not my fault. Having 5 kids and what accompanies that may have had a play there, but that was their decision, not mine.

I didn't want my mom to leave, and I am pretty certain I told her that. But I wasn't considerate of the fact that she must have been in pain to live in the same state as her children and had limited ability to spend time with them. I wasn't considerate of the fact all her adult life and her early teens had been dedicated to caring for her siblings and her children. My mom was the oldest of 12 at an early age, and my Nana relied on her to help with the family. My mom had not had a life of her own when she left us; she had married young and had kids young. She hadn't lived a life for herself. I had this resentment out of selfishness and fear. I was fifty-one before I realized how painful it must have been for her. My life was full of love from my wife, daughters, and others. I was holding on to a fear that I wasn't loved worthy enough; if I just opened my eyes, I would have seen differently.

I would finish off my resentment sheets and find that in all but a couple of instances, I had a role in my current feelings. I would also see that even though all these resentments started out as true, they were no longer true by the time I set them to paper. My mind had polished these things to the point where the story in my mind did not match what I had on paper. It was amazing the relief I felt, and I had just begun; it was time for my fears worksheet.

The fears worksheet is very similar to the resentments worksheet. The instructions are again listed in the Big Book step by Step. Fear is one of those emotions we learn and are not necessarily born with. We learn fear as we grow up as our basic instincts of life evolve. I would learn to be fearful when my parents argued, or when things didn't go as I planned them. After all there are really only three categories of fear when you boil it down. There's the fear that I might not get something I really want, like a better relationship or a good job. The fear of losing something I already have like my family or my own life. Then there's the fear you might find out something about me I don't care for you to know and then what will you think of me. When it comes to fears, like my resentments, I didn't think I really had any. But again, everyone has fears; it is a natural part of life. Fear is at the root of every negative feeling. If you are angry, you have a fear involved; if you are jealous, you have a fear involved. President Franklin D. Roosevelt said it best when he said, "The only thing we have to fear is fear itself." If I got stuck here, I referred back to my resentments sheet, and I looked for any place I had checked the box relating to fear. I asked myself what I was afraid of. I would list my fears, and some of the top ones would be liquor, being alone, death, failure, and not being liked. Again, these are just the top few; there were many others.

I would look at each fear and ask why I was afraid and what part of the self (basic instincts) I was relying on that had failed me. Liquor- I was afraid of booze. Now, I have had a taste of the good life, and I know booze can destroy that. I had always relied on my pride when it came to booze. I also tied booze to my emotional security. I thought I was strong enough to express my pride. But the reality was I was afraid of what my life would be without booze; how would that impact my personal relationships if I didn't have it? So it was my self-esteem I was protecting, not my pride.

The only thing I have changed is myself and my dependence on me. That today is in my higher power's hands. I depend on God to give me the strength I need. Liquor is not a thought today, and all I did was turn it over.

I don't fear death anymore. I don't look forward to it, but I know it is a part of life, the price of admission. If I don't enjoy the day, live in, and for the day, I'm already dead. Everybody is going to die, and I am no exception, but today I have life. I feared being alone. Now, of all the things I have written so far, this one is the most ironic for me. I feared being alone, despite the fact I always isolated myself from everyone, both physically and emotionally, so I could drink how I wanted to. Yet the thought of having nobody to isolate from was scary. My pride told me you'll always have someone, while my self-esteem told me you're not good enough to always have someone. I don't fear this anymore. If I treat people well, I am certain there will be someone by my side when I leave this world. When I leave this world, I will still have God by my side the way he is this very minute. I will never be alone.

That leaves failure because of my ego and my ambitions. I feared failure more than anything else. Failing for me was the ultimate defeat. But was that really true? I had failed to graduate High School, but because I had the drive to do better, I would learn from others and become as successful as anyone I knew. To fail is simply to not be successful on an attempt, but failure offers us so much. We learn from our failures. We learn what not to do the next time and seek out better paths to get to success. This was an imagined fear; there was no basis at all for me to have had this fear. A fear that would make it convenient for me to drink.

Once again, I would see my fears like my resentments were not as they seemed in my head. That they were only in my head so I could nurture them as my fallback for having a drink. Most of these fears were lies to me, but they were there.

We all fear things: success, failure, sickness, heights, and darkness. It is natural, but when the fear of heights stops you from being able to go to the office to work, or the fear of darkness keeps you from leaving the house after sunset, you better talk about that because that fear has evolved into a lie in your mind. Think about it: Why should I be angry today over what happened between my mother and father or even my friends and coaches for something that really happened 40 years ago. What real fears are actually there today? None of that can hurt me today unless I use it to hurt myself. It's kind of sadistic when you really think about it. I have learned today that when I feel a negative feeling, I need to find the fear involved; there's always a fear. It's only then that I can look at that fear and see it for what it is. I can make my decisions easier by understanding what fear or pain I am willing to live with. I used to have a fear of what others thought about me; today, I don't care what others think about me. That's their business. It is simply what I think about myself, and if I live a life without unnecessary fears, I feel pretty damn good about myself.

After my resentments and fears sheets were done, I only had one more to do, and that was my harm done to others. The funny thing is that a lot of the names on my resentment sheet ended up on my harms sheet. My mom was on my harms sheet. I had caused some of those beatings she took by telling my dad some of the things she had asked me not to do. My mom had a boyfriend or two over time, and when Dad asked where we had been, I told him. I was on my harms sheet, not just for my drinking but for not allowing myself to be me. I had stood in the way of growing because I was afraid to succeed or fail. Simply, I was afraid to try. I saw that even though the scenery had changed, all the actors were the same.

I would eventually need to ask for forgiveness from all who were on this sheet. My wife, daughters, and a lot of other people. But first, I would need to understand, as I did with resentments, the feelings behind my actions, and I would need to forgive myself for some bad decisions. I had gone through life for a very, very long time, only paying attention to what I wanted and never considering what I needed. Sure, we can all say that a want is the same as a need, but is it?

In my adult years, I had everything I ever needed. Yes, I would lose some things, but that was again through bad thinking. But I always wanted more and felt I had the right to it. But none of it ever seemed to fill this emptiness inside me. If I could only have that car, that would make me feel better, or if I only had that job, it would make me feel better. Maybe if I made more money and had more toys, that would make me feel better. But none of it ever did, maybe because in the sense of material things, I was already full, no room for more.

The third step actually gave me the one thing that made me feel whole. I had a great family already, made good money already, and had the freedom to do fun things already, but there was always this emptiness that only alcohol could seem to satisfy. But that came with a price, a heavy price. The third step led to my spirituality and my comfort in my own skin; it gave me a God of my own understanding.

After looking over my fourth step, I could see these things I was holding onto were just another way of filling the emptiness. Negative feelings take up as much space as positive feelings. I saw for the first time ever, these negative feelings had been taking up so much space inside me and not paying any rent or having any positive results. I needed to evict these things. After all, nothing I could do would ever change the actions of the past. But by letting good come into that space, I could change the way I saw the past. I could, for the first time, be considerate towards other people's situations. My Mom was a great, loving person, and my Dad was a great, loving person, but those negatives I held onto didn't allow me to see that. But now I had a higher power, a God who gave me the strength and clear vision to see how things really were.

Today, I have no resentments. If there is something that comes up that I don't like, I talk about it, I am honest about my feelings, and I deal with it. The funny thing is people really care about how other people feel. I never knew that. I had always lived with a victim mentality; it was me against the world in a way.

Having seen all this through my fourth step, I would pray about it and arrange to talk to my sponsor about these things. I was ready for Step 5.

Up until this time, I had worried about doing this step. I feared what my sponsor might think of me after hearing this stuff; I had actually thought, "he doesn't need to know everything." I am glad I never acted on those thoughts. My sponsor and I would meet at a local lighthouse, and he would let me go through my inventory. From time to time, he would stop me and ask me a question or two; if he felt that maybe my perception was off (which it was a lot), he would talk through the parts I was seemingly mixed up on. He and I would sit in the parking lot in my truck for over four hours.

It was the most amazing experience of my life, second to the birth of my children. I went from not wanting to tell him everything to not being able to shut up about any of it. I had never been more honest than that day up until that point, and honestly, it felt so freeing. It was this experience that showed me honesty was indeed the best policy. It showed me that truth does set me free. It is because of this step I try to live as honest of a life as I can. Four hours felt like one. I felt myself feeling cleaner and cleaner.

When we were done and I headed home, I remember calling my wife and telling her just how amazing I felt, how free I felt. I can only imagine what she must have thought on that call. I must have sounded crazy. I wasn't yet a year sober, but the feeling at that moment was like I had never even had a drink or a drinking problem.

The slate was clean, but the fifth step revealed work still to be done. I had to look at the things Dean and I had spoken about. Not the granular parts but the overlaying commonalities that seemed to tie each of those things together. This would be taken care of in Steps 6 and Step 7. Looking at each line on my resentments and the columns that had the basic instincts of life, I would see a common trend. I would see in each instance my self-esteem was checked, my personal relationships checked, sometimes my pride, sometimes my wallet.

These would be the things that were important to me to feel good. I would also see in the far column where I had been dishonest, inconsiderate, selfish, and made decisions based on fear. These would be the things that made me feel terrible. In Step 6, I would look at the things that made me feel bad and ask if I liked that about myself. The truth is I don't believe anyone likes to be dishonest. I doubt anyone likes to live in fear. I've never heard anyone say, "I am inconsiderate and damn proud of it." So, asking myself was a formality, but I had to do it; remember, I am dealing with my mind here, and my mind needs convincing.

In Step 7, I would pray for each negative feeling or defect of character to be removed and the opposite put in its place. This, for me, is an ongoing process. I will never be perfectly honest; I will always be a little selfish, but if I can be a little better today than I was yesterday, my life will continue to get better. As for the things that were important to me, my self-esteem? I do esteemable things like being honest and dependable. In my relationships, I apply the same logic. It works here, also. You know what I've found? It is much easier work to do the right things than it was to do what I used to do. As a result of improving on my character defects like dishonesty, being inconsiderate, selfishness, and fear. The things I saw as important to me in my fourth step, like my relationships, self-esteem, and ambitions, all got better without any real effort. I only needed to work on my negatives. The rest fell into place once I did.

I also had to review my fourth step, my inventory, so I could see all the people I had harmed. Step 8 requires I become willing to make amends to them all. See, once again, there's that word "willing." When I got here, I knew I had to set things straight with everyone. I owed it to them, but more importantly, I owed it to myself. But there were some people on this list that I was overly excited to set things right with. I would work with my sponsor, Dean, and we would break the list up into sections: the easier ones, a bit tougher ones, and the no f*#!ing way am I ever going to ones.

But I would get through them all; as I did the easy ones, the hardest didn't seem so challenging anymore. The feeling one gets from coming clean is amazing. Most of the people I would seek forgiveness from didn't even recall the incident in question. Most congratulated me on my sobriety and wished me well. They all probably thought, "About damn time." We can all make a living amends, and in some cases, that's really all we can do. Direct amends sometimes create more harm than good; in those cases, we find a different way.

In the end, we owe for all of our wrongdoings, and by not addressing them, we will still carry the guilt that may lead us to relapse. We do not make these amends for others; we make them for ourselves so we can be free of the guilt we carry in our minds so we can live a peaceful, sober life. Sponsors can help us with some of the more complicated cases; they've been in our shoes and can best guide us through the process. Making amends can be a lifelong process, but the dividends while doing the work are beyond anything you can imagine.

By this point in my sobriety, I had experienced so many positive results from applying these steps into my life I no longer needed to be convinced. As I mentioned in my podium speech, the first nine steps of this program are like cleaning the trash out of your life. The feeling of starting with a clean slate again is like being reborn. I have never in my life experienced anything like it.

Before I go any further, up to this point, this has been about me and my experience. But let me tell you about some of my AA friends and theirs.

First is my friend Jamie, you know, the one I spoke of earlier who said it takes a village. Jamie is slightly younger than I am; she would argue the word slightly. She came into recovery younger than some. She first felt cheated out of her drinking years. Jamie knew what an alcoholic life was like, but that itself didn't stop her from becoming one herself. A lot of her family members are in recovery. She grew up knowing what recovery was; she had her own perception of AA, but she understood the benefits of AA. Jamie is an intelligent person. She has a great personality. She makes friends easily and always has. She also has an annoying habit of trying to rescue every hurt animal she sees, but that's a story for another day.

She was a paramedic until she lost her job due to her drinking. That's not all she lost; she lost her car, her boyfriend, and most of all, her respect. She came into the halls around 9 months after me, she dove in, she had the gift of desperation. She got a sponsor, worked the steps of recovery, went to meetings, and actively participated in her recovery. She was one of those ladies who sat in the meeting, seemingly not paying attention as she knitted. But she was paying attention; somehow, knitting helped her concentrate on what was being said. But seriously, knitting?

Today, Jamie has great sobriety; she has a good life. She is still the person she was before, but today, she's comfortable enough with who she is that she allows everyone else to know that Jamie. She sponsors other people through the program of recovery. She is involved in her homegroup, and she is involved in service. Because she put her recovery first, today she has a new career, a career where she is trusted to manage other people. She has a brand new car that she recently purchased after building her credit and savings up. She now lives with the same boyfriend she lost through her drinking and is devoted to her relationship.

More importantly, she has her self-esteem and self-respect back. She had always been smart and driven, but that was never allowed to come to the surface; her disease held that back. Her disease used fear to hold her down to hold her back. If you were to ask her today, she would probably tell you that her life is better than she could have imagined.

My friend John came in and out of AA for a few years. Always coming in to get people off his back. He did not see himself as an alcoholic, he never worked the steps. He thought he could deal with his disease on his own. But one night, heading home after a night of heavy drinking, John gets into a car accident. He would leave the scene but be tracked down by the local police and the TV crew from Live PD. John was a young guy just having fun, he thought.

But that night would change his life. The world would know of his drinking now. He was on TV, and everyone would know. He feared losing his job. He was already on shaky ground with his family and his girlfriend. He could no longer see himself as nonalcoholic. But he had a number in his phone of a person he had met in AA. He was finally desperate enough to call that number. That call would set forward his journey into a sober life. John would meet with that AA member, and they would share their stories with each other; John could identify with what he had heard. John had always seen himself as fun, the center of attention. John was and still is a great, confident guy; just ask him, and he'll tell you. But he would do things while drinking, so he was the center of attention.

John also enjoys a nice life today. He is a solid member of AA, and he also sponsors people seeking sobriety. He married that girlfriend he was on shaky ground with, and they recently had a son. John had a problem with God at first. Which is understandable. I mean, you can't be the center of attention when God is. So, he had to become humble enough to allow God into his life. John was always a loving, caring person; he just never felt comfortable enough with himself to let the real John shine through.

There are so many people who have had similar experiences, like John and Jamie. The details are all different, but the results are the same. Completing the first nine steps of recovery allows you to see what parts of yourself you have been relying on to drink, so today you can stay sober. Nobody chooses to be an alcoholic. I never once spoke to an alcoholic who had become an alcoholic on their top ten list of things to do when they were growing up.

There are a lot of different contributing factors that create the perfect storm to be an alcoholic. Many, if not most, of them come in the way we end up seeing ourselves and the people around us. The ability to be the victim in any circumstance. The world is not out to get us; we just feel like it is, and our mind sees it that way. If you have honestly completed the first nine steps of recovery, your view has changed by this point. You have come to understand that although some of your thoughts and feelings may have started out as truth, today they are a lie, and you could never see the truth. That is the part of my podium speech that refers to sanity. But now that you have cleaned up your feelings from the past, how do you make sure you don't get back to that bad space? That is where the last three steps of recovery come in.

Where steps 4,5,6,7,8,9 had helped clean up our past, Step 10, "Continued to take personal inventory and when we were wrong promptly admitted it." would be what I would need to have an ongoing way of living that would deliver the same results those six steps in a single step. If I continue to take my personal inventory daily, I can make certain that the truth of today doesn't become the lie of tomorrow. Admitting I am wrong is not a weakness, it is a strength. If everyone in this world was perfect, by definition, everyone would be average. If I have learned anything in the first nine steps, it has been I am who I am, and nobody is going to accept me as I am if I don't first accept myself and all my deficiencies. If I work on my defects, accept myself, and respect the fact that others have different thoughts than I do, I shouldn't have much on my daily list. But if I have something on my step ten inventory, I better address it, or I am liable to relapse.

Step 11 is a living step, "Sought through prayer and meditation to improve our conscious contact with God as we understood Him, praying only for knowledge of His will for us and the power to carry that out." This is a step I take every day. Something I never did at all when I was drinking. When I was drinking, my alcoholic disease decided what my will would be. Remember, in Step 3, "will" simply means our thinking. In steps two and three, I would do what step eleven lays out.

Steps ten and eleven are the in-the-day steps, the steps that help me live my life today. The first nine steps are designed to help clear up my understanding of the past and understand myself a little better. Steps 10,11 and 12 are the living steps I apply to my everyday life, if I want to continue my sober life. If I have truly decided that I am not God, that I need to rely on a higher power to help me, then step eleven is simple; I had been living in this step as I was going through the process of the earlier steps. The final three steps actually had become a part of my life long before I took step four. I had seen what living in 10, 11, and 12 had done for the other alcoholics in my meetings. They would help me learn how to see things and how to understand my feelings before I experienced the steps that would show me what I needed to know about myself. What those other alcoholics were actually doing was part of their twelfth step. They helped me understand there was hope. They had become my family, and they still are today.

I have been an active member, a proud member of Alcoholics Anonymous for over eight years as of the writing of this book. From time to time, I get asked if I still need to go to meetings based on my time in sobriety; the real answer is yes. I know what my life used to be like. I have been around the halls of AA long enough to have witnessed what happens to others when they stop going to meetings and doing the things that support their sobriety. They relapse, time after time they relapse. I can't state with 100% certainty that I would relapse, but I am not willing to take that chance. The truth is I know what it was like before my sobriety. I know the feelings. I know the despair.

I also know that when people come into sobriety, they feel better; they reach a point where they have never felt as good as they do at that moment. Their thoughts are that they have arrived, and everything in their life has started to come back together. What they don't know, what they don't consider, is that it gets even better. My life is better today than it was last year; despite the ups and downs life throws at me, I have been able to handle them. That is because of my program, which I am certain about. I believe that having my meetings is a blessing. I have people who have recovered from the same sickness that I have. Our thinking is more aligned as we understand how an alcoholic mind thinks.

Doesn't matter if an alcoholic is actively drinking or not, to be able to fall victim to our old way of thinking. Our disease is never cured. We get a daily reprieve from our symptoms, provided we take our medicine.

Let me paint a picture for you. My niece is a diabetic; nobody thinks anything of it. But if she doesn't take care of her disease, she becomes very ill. Taking care of diabetes is simple as an outsider. You have to take your readings, take your insulin, and monitor your diet. For a diabetic, it's not that easy. My niece was a young child when she was diagnosed with diabetes; that was like being labeled lame. No real trick or treating and feasting on chocolate until you burst. Constantly needing to have your finger pricked to get blood for your readings three times a day. Then another needle in either your leg or butt, depending on which area you were giving a rest due to the constant injections required. My niece is in her thirties today, over 25,000 shots of insulin later, over 25,000 finger pricks later, and today, she is still a diabetic and will still need to repeat that process tomorrow if she wants to stay healthy. If she stops taking her insulin, family members will worry and wonder what she could be thinking.

As an alcoholic, I am faced with a similar situation. My disease cannot be cured either. Instead of a combined 1,200 finger pricks and insulin needles a year, I attend around 120 meetings a year. Everyone would be appalled if a diabetic stopped taking their insulin, their medicine. But an alcoholic wonders if they still need theirs. How could that even be a question? Without the actions that got me sober, I would still be that drunk. If the actions I took were the medicine I needed to not be sick anymore, why would I think going back to a life without my medicine would result in anything other than relapse.

As I mentioned earlier, my dad died from cancer. He had undergone radiation treatment for his cancer. He was feeling better, getting stronger. He decided to take on chemo, and that would be the beginning of the end. My dad was willing to risk it all for the opportunity to be healthier. I often think of this when I consider what I had to do to be healthier. In the grand scheme of things, what I had to do was nothing. My dad had a willingness to do whatever it took to rid himself of cancer. I also had a willingness to do whatever I needed to do to be free from the bondage of my addiction, so on that level, we were even. But what I had to do was far less dangerous, far less dangerous than what my dad decided to do. But in both instances, we both had a willingness to do whatever it took to be better and feel better.

My recovery today is just as dependent on my willingness as it was on day one. But today, that willingness is based on faith, not hope. When I first went to an AA meeting, I had hoped that it would help me. I saw how others seemed, and they seemed happy. The people in the halls poked fun at their misadventures and laughed at themselves. They didn't have that shame I felt, that feeling of being lost in the woods without a compass. They gave me the hope I needed that I could also have what they had. After all my time and all the things life has thrown my way and never needing to take a drink to get through it, I have faith that this program works.

I once worked with a newcomer to recovery. His name was Brendon. Brendon was a young guy; his drinking had driven his marriage to divorce. I visited Brendon in the hospital one day. He was recovering from his latest drinking spree. Brendon had been held over at the hospital because he suffered from pancreatitis as a result of his drinking. The physical pain he was in was incredible. He had been told that drinking would only make matters worse, and yet here he was again. Brendon and I set a plan for when he was released to get to work on his program. I was committed. He was not. When Brendon was released, I visited his home. He was laid out on the couch in pain.

When he had been released from the hospital, his pain had been manageable, and if he had stayed away from a drink, it would improve with time. When I visited him and saw his condition, I asked him what had happened. He explained to me that he had been uncomfortable and the only thing that would relieve the pain was to drink. Despite the fact he knew that drinking would actually worsen his condition overall, the doctors told him that yet he relied on the brief relief he thought he got. That's insane! It's like trying to put a fire out with gasoline. Brendon would never finish his steps; he would go back out, and I haven't seen him again.

Brendon was simply not willing to see the truth from the false. His obsession with drinking would overcome all reasonable thinking. This is the truth we all need to consider; our minds will always try to convince us a drink won't hurt us when we know it will. How can that type of thinking be called anything other than insane?

I had another sponsee, Eric. Eric came in after being involved in a car accident. He had his young son in the car when this happened. Eric loves his son very, very much.

Eric had to take a job at a nearby gas station as he had lost his right to drive as a result of that accident. His earning potential had been greatly impacted. He had split from his wife, the mother of his son, as a result of his drinking. When Eric came to AA, he was desperate to put his life back together, and he started taking suggestions. He became active in his recovery program and worked the steps of recovery. Eric's life started to get better. He was able to see his son more frequently. After the accident, the mom understandably restricted those visits. He would regain his right to drive with a breathalyzer installed in his car.

Eric would complete his steps, but for Eric, it was a one-and-done thing. He failed to carry forward what had made his life better. Eric would reach one year sober anniversary; in his mind, he had crossed the finish line. Eric would relapse; he knew he couldn't drink alcohol, so he would drink cough syrup. The breathalyzer couldn't detect the cough syrup; this was a planned event. He would argue that point, but on what grounds? He knew the breathalyzer was in his car. He knew it couldn't detect the cough syrup. He had bottles and more bottles of cough syrup both in his car and in his home. He hadn't been sick in the sense of a cold or flu. Why the need for so much cough syrup?

Eric fell victim to a thought process so many do; if he didn't need alcohol over the past year, he had been cured. This is a common thing we who have addictive traits seem to fall for. Having stayed away from alcohol for some set amount of time, we feel we can go back to it without the same results as they had experienced before.

I am an alcoholic. I will always be an alcoholic. My body assures me I cannot drink without losing control of how much I drink. Not only does the Big Book of Alcoholics Anonymous tell me this, but so does science. I know as I sit here today, my body cannot metabolize alcohol. Thus, I know if I had even one drink, it would require I have another and another, and I'll end up drunk all over again. When I got sober, my favorite dessert was tiramisu; it was my go-to anytime I went out to eat. I don't eat tiramisu in restaurants anymore. Most recipes for tiramisu use alcohol. Now, would the amount of alcohol in a desert be enough to activate the body's allergy? I don't know, and I am not willing to find out. There are always plenty of other options on the menu that are just as tasty as tiramisu and have zero risk of triggering a relapse. If I want tiramisu, I can make it myself at home, and I know it will be safe.

Before I got sober, I went to a lot of NFL football games. I tailgated and usually got so drunk at the tailgate party that I didn't remember the game the next day. When I got sober, I wasn't willing to give up going to games and partying before the game. I still go to games, I still tailgate, I just don't drink booze. You wanna know what I found out? The games are actually more fun sober; the stadiums actually give coupons for free soda and other non-alcoholic drinks if you identify yourself as a designated driver, which I always am. I actually remembered the game I spent over $200 per ticket on; it was pretty amazing.

I don't do all the things I did while I was drinking, but almost everything I cut out wasn't really fun. I did it so I could drink. I've been to bachelor parties, stayed until everyone was reaching the point of drunken annoyance, and then left. Business events are a part of my normal life; people know I don't drink, and I always excuse myself when my need to be there is done.

I look back on my drunken life as a period of learning. I am not proud of my actions, but today, I know I wouldn't do today what I did when I was drinking. I am a different person today. Sometimes, people in sobriety live in their past. I think that's a mistake. I clearly have not forgotten my past; I just choose not to live there. I can learn from the past so I can have a better today, but that's all the past has to offer me. If I had spent today living yesterday, then I would have wasted another day I could have enjoyed.

We cannot be in two places at the same time, so if I am always caught up in the person I used to be, I can never become the person I was intended to be. Setting my expectations is always dangerous, but if they are based on a false premise, like who I used to be, then that is built on a lie. My past life was always a lie; who I pretended to be to you was a lie. Most of the things I thought I wanted were lies.

The fact I got pissed off over my parents splitting up, lie. I would lay awake in bed as the fights were going on, praying for them to split up; that's what I really wanted at that moment. I have spent a lifetime building some fictional tale based on what others thought of me and told me who and what I should be.

I was an actor in my relationships, playing the role I needed to be accepted by you. If someone in my life liked fishing, I liked fishing. If another person in my life thought fishing was terrible, I thought fishing was terrible. I was who I needed to be based on the audience. It never occurred to me I could be liked for just being me. I thought I had to act like you, be like you, so that you would like me.

My life was based on my perception of everyone, not reality. I did things because of what I thought others would think of me. That's crazy. I couldn't read minds then, and I am not any better at that today. Yet I knew what you thought of me? People would have accepted me for who I was if I had given them a chance to know the real me. The problem was I was never comfortable enough in my own skin and therefore, not comfortable with you knowing the real me. It was me who was judging you, not the other way around.

Not everything in my life was a lie. My marriage was never a lie. I have always loved my wife and adored her. I was just never very good at showing it. I had no role models that I could mold what a good relationship should look like in my life. The love for my children was as real as it gets. My ambition to be successful was real. Almost everything else seemed to be a mirage. The best lies we tell ourselves have to have some element of truth in them. We build our lives on falsehoods in one fashion or another. If we didn't, we wouldn't need to drink or take drugs. Sometimes, we carry those skills into early sobriety.

Today, I trust people; I let them "in." In my third year of sobriety, I would get an offer to sell my business. This offer would come from someone I respected, but nonetheless, it was scary. I had spent the better part of my life building this company; it was part of my identity. Every other day, I would have a different answer. One day, I was ready to sell; the next, I didn't want to sell. One day, I said no to the offer.

My good friend Tom, who I consider my business mentor today, responded with, "You should first know what you're saying no to." He was right! I would come to understand the offer, and fear would be in the way, but now I recognized the fear. I was afraid of the unknown. What would it look like if I sold? I already knew what it looked like not selling. I would need to get comfortable with the fact I am not any better at seeing the future than I was at reading minds. I sold my company to my friend Tom, and I still work for him today. I am grateful to him for not letting me just say no. He has become a dear and trusted friend. I would have never associated with someone like Tom before. After all he's a Harvard Graduate, has a brilliant business mind, and pretty ok people skills. I trust people today. That's pretty amazing.

I have another friend, her name is Sabby. I met Sabby in detox at AdCare. She came in on my second day. Sabby was this meek girl. When she came in, she had this oversized hoodie and kept her head low. She was scared to be there. Her hands shook from the DTs and some of that fear. We would sit for hours doing a puzzle together, talking as though we knew each other. The reality is we knew each other because we were both alcoholics. Sabby would be the first friend I would make in sobriety. I got out of detox on a Monday. I gave Sabby my number to call me when she got out. Sabby would call me when she got out of detox. We started talking every Tuesday night, usually when I was on my way to my new AA meeting, you know, the one I spoke about in my opening podium speech.

Sabby had tried a couple AA meetings; she didn't talk to anyone nor join a group. I would tell her how I was doing and how AA was helping me feel better and not think about drinking.

Shortly after I passed the six-month mark, Sabby called me to tell me she "slipped." She was drunk, she was depressed, and she relapsed. Sabby didn't slip, as she put it; she wanted to drink more than she wanted to be sober. She had, in that moment, forgotten all the pain she had been through. This would begin a series of drinking events for Sabby; she hadn't resorted to daily drinking, at least I don't think she did. We would still talk every week; often, I could tell she had been drinking. I often spoke to my sponsor because I didn't know what to do. All he would say is just be there for her. One night, Sabby told me she had figured out how to handle this drinking thing. She had a "plan." She told me if she could have her husband pour her drinks, she believed she would be fine. That was so insane I sat for a minute, dumbfounded at what I had just heard.

Having been in AA for a little over six months at this point, I had been working my steps and had read a bit of the Big Book, but now I was experiencing the lack of sanity the book spoke of firsthand. At that moment, I did what I thought I needed to do. It was painful, like my heart and soul being ripped from my body, but I told Sabby she had to go back out and drink, as clearly she hadn't hit bottom yet. I almost cried as I said the words, but it needed to be said.

It's the tale of two alcoholics. We had both started in detox, where we met. One would get out and instantly go to AA meetings, join a homegroup, and become the coffee maker of that group. The other would dip her toes in the water of AA, go to a couple meetings, stand or sit in the back of the room, not really talk to anyone in the meetings, and leave right after the meetings. One would get a sponsor and start working on the steps. My sponsor would give me CDs of Joe and Charlie to help me understand the steps. The other still hadn't spoken to anyone at a meeting when and if she went. One would be working on his fourth step, going to commitments as a part of his twelfth step. The other was thinking of ways to control her drinking while drinking.

Their life outside of AA was similar; both were happily married, and both were employed in jobs they liked. In fact, Sabby had just started working at a job that she felt she deserved. It's funny what happens when an alcoholic gets what they want before they have done any work on themselves to deserve it.

Sabby would go back to drinking, and she would eventually lose that job she deserved. She Would hit her bottom after a few months. We would still talk every week. That hadn't changed. Then, one day, during one of our talks, she told me she was going back into rehab. She was going out of state for a long-term program. While Sabby was in rehab, I would still call her every Tuesday. She didn't have access to her phone in rehab, so I knew I wouldn't reach her, but I would leave a message each time so she knew I was pulling for her.

Sabby is sober today with some years under her belt. She and her husband recently bought a new home; they have an oasis as a backyard. Her life is better; she is happy. I am happy for her.

Chapter 04

SEEING THE FACTS

We all walk a different path; sometimes, we trip and fall. It's not about how many times you fall down. It's about how many times you are willing to get back up. I have learned a lot about myself during my journey, and I still have a lot more to learn. Addiction will kill you, but only if you decide to let it. There is a solution; there is hope. What lengths are you willing to go to for a better life? Someone once asked, when do you know you've hit bottom? My answer is you hit bottom when you decide to stop digging. When you're ready to fight for your right to be sober and give up the fight for your right to drink.

A change of perception is needed, a change of priorities is needed, and a change of Gods is required. Your God today is your drink or the drug you are willing to sacrifice everything for right now. We all know it in our hearts. We sacrifice our families for our drinking. We sacrifice our financial well-being for a drink. We sacrifice our reputations, our professional standing, and anything else that stands between us and our drink.

If you decide you want to get sober, then there is a solution waiting for you. People who understand, people who care, people who have been in your shoes. At the beginning of this book, I speak of truth. And the two words that are synonymous with truth, fact, and reality. So, let's look at the facts of the most effective program of recovery.

It would all start in 1935 with two alcoholics; within a couple years, they would have forty who had become sober. By 1939, there were one hundred sober. That's a growth rate of 5,000%. By 1976, there were over one million sober; in 2013, over two million sober in over 150 countries.

Numbers do not lie. The program of recovery is not a passing fad, with over 2.1 million members today, and an estimated 23 million sober curious. Recovery will work for you if you are willing to do the work. AA has survived all these years with the program unchanged. I cannot think of a single thing or program that has remained the same for nearly ninety years and maintained a high rate of success other than AA.

Now, if you go the route I have traveled, I want to tell you some misinformation you may hear. The first one is "There are no musts in AA." That's not true if you are looking to be successful. First of all, there are 103 musts in the Big Book Of Alcoholics Anonymous. The AA Preamble states, "The only requirement for membership is a desire to stop drinking," a requirement is a must. Another fable is you can have anything you want as your higher power.

While it is true that AA is not a religious organization, the idea that you can have a light bulb or a chair as a higher power is plain ludicrous thinking. Step 3 asks you to turn your will and your life over to that higher power. If I had a problem with turning my life over to God, do you really think a light bulb or a chair would do anything for me? Does the suggestion in step 11 mean that I seek to improve my conscious contact with a chair and do that through prayer to the chair. The last one I will talk about is the one some say that the steps will make you drink. No, that's the biggest lie of them all. If you drink when doing the steps, it's fear that is making you drink, not the steps that have gotten millions sober.

It is always important to keep in mind that AA was born through alcoholics created by alcoholics, not doctors or what we know as recovery professionals. AA is made up of millions of alcoholics who all have their own personalities involved. Each group in AA looks different. A different format, a different set of rules, that is known as the group conscience. That in itself is a recipe for controversy.

This controversy over time however has proven to be a positive thing; it is what has allowed the program to evolve and keep current with the times. No one group is better or worse than the next. What it does is to allow for a new person looking to get sober, to find a group they feel comfortable with. Whether it be the format of the meeting or the people in the meeting. Today, there is something for everyone.

It wasn't like that in the early days; very few meetings existed, and there was no variety. Now, it may seem as though I am saying it is easier today than it was in the early days of AA; in some ways, it is, but in others, it's harder today.

Today, we have stuff like social media and the internet. If we want to feel insufficient, social media will definitely help us confirm that. Just go out there, and you get to see just how everyone else's life is so great while yours may seem to suck. Or just share an idea or a thought or even an honest opinion and have dozens of comments about why you don't know what you're talking about. If we want access to information or find the latest gadget we want to buy, the internet fills that need. No need to socialize, go to the library to research things, or go to shopping centers to buy things. Just isolate in our rooms and have everything delivered to our door, even our booze.

They didn't have to deal with any of that in the thirties and forties. The freedom to use drugs today is more accepted than ever, and certain drugs are being legalized, paving the way for even more deadly drugs to come to market.

That also wasn't anything they contended with in the early days. Some things were much easier back then, while other things like fellowship, worksheets, and understanding were not as easy. As I said earlier, alcoholism and addiction are as old as time itself, and today, it looks as bad as it did centuries ago for the active alcoholic. The difference today is there is a way out.

Today, we live in a world of instant gratification; we no longer live by the old expression, "Anything worth having is worth waiting for." An article in Psychology Today talks about delayed gratification being a battle worth winning. It is likened to a person believing they are incapable of mowing their lawn because he or she does not understand how to use their lawnmower. They will never mow the lawn as long as they think they cannot do it. However, if the person realizes that they just need to learn how to use their lawn mower, eventually they learn and mow the lawn.

The same is true for the suffering alcoholic and our choice preferences. Our lawnmowers work. We just need to learn how to use them. As an alcoholic, we want the smaller immediate rewards a drink brings to us regardless of the fact it is not long-lasting or permanent. Rather than focus on the larger payoff and more permanent solution offered through sobriety. We choose short bursts of relief, followed by deeper pain when we come out of our drunken state. Our life is filled with more and more feelings of unmanageability, requiring more frequent and heavier drinking. Again, it is like trying to put a fire out with gasoline.

I cannot tell you if AA is for you. There are many ways to achieve sobriety. AA is the way I found the program that helped me. The recovery program of AA has also been recognized in a comprehensive analysis conducted by a Stanford School of Medicine researcher and his collaborators. Most of the studies that measured abstinence found AA was significantly better than other interventions or no intervention. In one study, it was found to be 60% more effective. None of the studies found AA to be less effective.

I also mentioned earlier that we have but two options in our alcoholism; one is to find a way to live our life without alcohol, and the other is to die from our disease. Another national study shows that every four minutes, a person dies because of alcoholism. Over 43,200 alcoholics have died during the time it took me to write this book; that is truly sad; they didn't have to die. The main purpose of this book is to show you that you are not alone and that there is hope if you want it.

When I set out to write this book, it was with one goal in mind: to save the life of an alcoholic. If this book accomplishes that, then it was all worth it. My book will never save as many lives as the Big Book of Alcoholics Anonymous, but hopefully, it will help save one. In my story that opened this book, I list some people I am grateful for; allow me to finish that list.

I am grateful to my Dr. Friend, who suggested AdCare to start with. Without that suggestion, I wouldn't be sober today. I am grateful for my wife, who has stuck by me through thick and thin, and without her, I don't know if I'd be sober or even alive today. In the beginning, my love for her and my daughters was my higher power. I am grateful to all the people in AA that have been there for me over the years. I have real friends today. What's not to be grateful for. I am grateful to the newcomer for helping keep me on track with my program. Working with someone new to sobriety is so rewarding. You actually get to see life come back into another person's eyes.

I am also grateful to two people I have never had the pleasure of meeting, Joe and Charlie. These are two older southern gentlemen who were very influential in my sobriety and sparked my interest in the Big Book. This is an app you can download from the Apple Store or from the Android Marketplace. These two guys studied the Big Book together and held Big Book study weekends. They break the book down so masterfully in a real person's way of doing things. I discussed earlier how I am not a big studier and never was. So when I saw that Big Book, I was a bit intimidated and

101

scared that I would need to really have to get over my fear and laziness if I was going to be successful.

My sponsor must have recognized that he gave me a CD set of Joe and Charlie to listen to. I listened to those CDs religiously, not just because I needed to but because I actually enjoyed listening to these two old-timers. I still listen to them today. They have a way of speaking that makes everything just make sense. If you are like me and not overly enthused about reading, I strongly suggest downloading the AA Joe and Charlie app. It costs less than a pint of Vodka, and the good feeling you'll get just listening to them will definitely last much longer.

I can only tell you of my experience in getting sober as well as the people whose stories I have shared a little about. All these stories are real, as are their experiences as they relate to their own recovery. The people in this book are real people, just like the readers of this book. I don't have any other worthwhile advice on any other program, as this is the only thing that has worked for me. I don't speak on behalf of AA but rather as a member who has been blessed with the gift promised in the program.

Eight years ago, I couldn't stop drinking even when I wanted to. I couldn't figure out why I couldn't stop. Over the years, my self-esteem was depleted. I was just going through the motions, happy on the outside, dying on the inside. Sobriety has delivered the serenity I needed to be as happy on the inside as I appear on the outside. My self-esteem has grown because I do esteemable acts like working with other alcoholics, helping the people in my life, and being honest with those people about my real feelings.

My homegroup in AA is named the Drunk Squad. It is not my original homegroup. My original homegroup was Age Doesn't Matter. I love that group as much as I love my current group. I joined Age Doesn't Matter on June 29th, 2015, and dove in the middle and became active in my own recovery. That was to be my forever group. Then the pandemic hit. Meetings started turning to Zoom. That wouldn't work for me. I needed and still need to be around real alcoholics person to person. There is something about being accountable that is important to my own sobriety. My homegroup was split on this matter. The pandemic has brought a lot of fear to the table for everyone across the country. This was a huge unknown that we were going through. Relapse rates were jumping; they were estimated to have jumped by 38% during the early days of the pandemic.

The pandemic offered a perfect storm for the borderline alcoholic or the on-the-fence recovering alcoholic. You had to isolate yourself; you could order your booze from restaurants; they even offered curbside pick up and delivery of your booze. Churches told some groups they could no longer use their church for meetings because of fear and the unknown. My group was split on the matter; some of us wanted to "keep the doors open" for the newcomer who may not find a Zoom meeting, and most members wanted to move to virtual meetings. Fear drove everyone's decisions. My fear of relapse drove my decision to meet face to face; others' fear drove them to the world of virtual meetings. There is no right or wrong here. As long as an alcoholic is working on their program of recovery, we protect ourselves from relapse.

I was one who wanted and needed in-person meetings. There was no wrong answer here. People have to do what is best for them, best for their sobriety. I didn't want to be a cause for controversy, but I needed to do what was best for my sobriety, so I started a new group, The Drunk Squad. People came. There were others who needed that in-person meeting as well. Last night, The Drunk Squad celebrated 3 years as a group. We had nearly 90 people at the meeting. This book is dedicated to the members of The Drunk Squad, among others. They helped save a lot of lives when others were losing theirs.

Many newcomers have found their sobriety at a time when so many who were sober found the bottle again.

People say they drink to escape things. I wouldn't argue if that was accurate or not. I do know, especially at the end of my drinking, the only thing I was escaping was myself. I had pretty much alienated myself from most people who actually cared about me. But it was that feeling of less than that I was running away from. Most of my hard drinking was done in isolation, so who was I really escaping if not myself. I don't need to escape today. I am able to face what life throws at me and deal with it.

Don't get me wrong, it is not always easy, but when it gets too hard, I have a fellowship to fall back on and guide me through the rough waters. I know what life is like to live as an active alcoholic. The feelings of hopelessness and despair. Feeling as though the world is out to get you, that you cannot catch a break. Always waiting for the next problem or latest bad news. That is what it is like. I know; I've lived it.

Today, I see yesterday from a different perspective. I had always fit in; I just didn't see it. I saw everyone trying to help me fit in as people feeling sorry for me. My parents always loved me. I just saw their actions wrong. I didn't understand the pain they themselves were going through. The world and all its people weren't out to get me. I'm just not that important for people to plan how to destroy my life. Today, I see that I saw the world the way I wanted to see it, a way that would justify my own actions.

Today, my spirituality does for me what alcohol used to do for me. The program of recovery hasn't just changed the way I see the world today, but it has changed my view of my past. Sobriety is much more than just not drinking. It is about having serenity in one's own skin. And yes, I credit that growth to my willingness to believe in a Higher Power, to believe in my own perception of God.

I have used the word God nearly 90 times in this book, but I want to be clear on something. I have spirituality, not religion. I don't really go to church unless there is an event like a wedding or baptism. I don't have anything against the church, but I also don't need to go to church to have found the God of my understanding.

There is a story I believe allowed me to have my understanding of God. There were the three Wiseman of the east, and they took from man the crown of life, the thing that would make us the happiest, and took it away from them. And they said, "Now that we took it away from them, what are we going to do with it?" One of them said I'll tell you what we'll do; we'll take it to the highest, highest crevice on the face of the earth in the highest, highest mountain, and we'll hide it up there, and they'll never be able to find it. And the other two said yeah, but you know how they are, they'll hunt, and they'll search, and they'll eventually find it. The second one said I'll tell you what, we'll take it to the deepest, deepest crevice of the deepest ocean and hide it there, and they'll never think about looking for it there. He said yeah, but you know how they are. They'll hunt, and they'll search, and they'll eventually find it. The third one said I'll tell you what we'll do; we'll hide it within himself, and he'll never think about looking for it there.

I can identify with that story. I never understood the concept of a higher power. I believed because I was taught to believe. What I believed in was someone else's conception of God, not my own. I didn't have a God of my own because I wasn't taught I could. My spirituality doesn't come from AA, but AA gave me permission to find my own spirituality. I do believe in a God and I always have, and my conception isn't too far off what some religions preach. You, too, can have your own God. It's as easy as writing down on a piece of paper what your God is. People say that I've found God, but that isn't true, as God was never lost. I was the one who was lost.

I have been fortunate in my life. I didn't always recognize it. When I was in my darkest days, consumed by my alcoholic disease, I still had people who loved me and cared about me. They only wanted me to get better, be happier, and live the life I intended to live. I didn't see that. I saw people judging me, not understanding me, and avoiding me. I saw some of the events in my past in a way that allowed me to feel justified in my drinking. I didn't see the good, only the bad. I didn't see my role in the way others responded to me. If I could have, I would have understood. If some of the people in my life had treated me in the ways I treated them, I would have done the same. My life is not perfect today. I am not perfect today. But I have a life I am comfortable with and enjoy. Life still throws shit my way, but life throws shit everybody's way. It's ironic how everyone in my life has seemed to change since I got sober. The only irony there is the fact I see it that way.

I am the only person that has undergone any sort of change. That's the reality. But that change hasn't just impacted the way I feel about myself. It impacts the way I feel about everyone. Words cannot express my gratitude for the opportunity to have this gift of sobriety. God knows I've used over 33,000 words in this book, and it still does not fully represent the feelings I have for life and being sober in life.

I have been fortunate. I have had the rare opportunity to live two lives in one lifetime. One is an active alcoholic. Suffering the pains that accompany that. A never-ending road to deep depression. Never felt good enough no matter how hard I tried, no matter how much I was really accepted. A life that was so painful I had to drink to get away from myself, drinking for oblivion. Not wanting to live, not wanting to die. A life I was only showing up as being present but never present enough to live life each day.

Today, I have a life of sobriety, a life that brings me true happiness. A life I get to enjoy all the good in my days like the birth of my grandson and grandchildren to come. Being part of my daughters' lives as they become successful women and start their lives. I will get to be there and enjoy the special moments as they get married, buy homes, have families, or just live their lives. I enjoy just sitting on the couch watching TV with my wife, engaging in trivial chit-chat as we grow old together. I enjoy the fellowship and my friends in AA. I also get to enjoy all the bad days, like sitting in traffic but knowing there is a reason for it. Maybe I just needed the time for reflection that being alone in a car can give me. I enjoy difficult people because they help me grow as a person as I navigate the waters of that encounter.

I wouldn't trade my best drinking days for my worst sober days. I am truly amazed at the change in me that has happened. I don't need to have all the answers today. What a relief. I am never the most important person in the room, which is another relief. Today, I enjoy the gift of having lived two lives within one lifetime. One as an active suffering alcoholic and the other as a sober recovering alcoholic. I choose sobriety; the question is, what will you choose?

I opened this book with my podium story, and I want to close it the way we close our meetings of The Drunk Squad with the last paragraph from a vision for you.

A Vision for You (pg. 164 Big Book)

Abandon yourself to God as you understand God. Admit your faults to Him and to your fellows. Clear away the wreckage of your past. Give freely what you find, and join us. We shall be with you in the Fellowship of the Spirit, and you will surely meet some of us as you trudge the Road of Happy Destiny.

May God bless you and keep you – until then.

Made in the USA
Middletown, DE
28 October 2023

41448767R00068